JESUS CHRIST
MOVIE STAR

By Phil Hall

Published in the USA by:
BearManor Media
1317 Edgewater Dr #110
Orlando, FL 32804
www.bearmanormedia.com

Paperback ISBN: 978-1-62933-698-5
Case ISBN: 978-1-62933-699-2
BearManor Media, Orlando, Florida
Printed in the United States of America
Book design by Robbie Adkins, www.adkinsconsult.com

Dedicated to the cherished memory of Rev. Dr. Forrest Church (1948 – 2009), who wisely observed: "None of us is fully able to perceive the truth that shines through another person's window, nor the falsehood that we may perceive as truth. Thus, we can easily mistake another's good for evil, and our own evil for good."

Advance Praise for Jesus Christ Movie Star

"Filmmakers have been telling the story of Jesus since the very inception of the cinema. Phil Hall gives true insight into this compelling history." – Lon Davis, film historian and author of *Silent Lives: 100 Biographies of the Silent Film Era*

"Through these pages you will be intrigued with the similarities and differences used by filmmakers to tell this timeless story. This thought-provoking book will provide you not only with a greater appreciation for film but also for the most pivotal character in history." – Judah Thomas, founder and lead pastor, Thrive Church

"Phil Hall once again combines wit and charm with thorough research to explore the depths of the cinema universe to trace the various ways Jesus Christ has appeared in film. In this charming work, he provides a thorough and fascinating history of the intersection between the deeply spiritual and entertainment in a manner that respects both the subject and the medium. The works covered vary from the niche to the widely-known, and there is enough to interest both the novice and the expert alike." – Jeffrey Peters, PhD, scholar at Catholic University of America and publisher/editor of *The News and Times*

"If 'God created man in His own image' (the Bible) and 'If God did not exist, it would be necessary to invent him' (Voltaire), then each generation has remade God to suit its time and place. It's the theme Phil Hall explores in this cleverly titled book about the complex history of Jesus Christ on the big screen. Whether you're a believer – in Jesus as God or the cinema, for that matter – you'll be engaged by the way Hall blends his passion for film and his Christian faith with his gifts for smooth storytelling and quirky detail." – Georgette Gouveia, editor-in-chief, *WAG Magazine.*

Table of Contents

Author's Note

*"But beyond this, my son, be warned: the writing of many books is
endless, and excessive devotion to books is wearying to the body."*
– *Ecclesiastes* 12:12

During the creation of this book, I was approached by Rich Cyr,
a writer and actor who is my co-host on the weekly syndicated
radio talk show *Nutmeg Junction*.

"Hey, Phil, I've got a film for your book!" Rich exclaimed. "Have
you ever heard of *Jesus Christ: Serial Rapist*?"

Amazingly, this was one title that managed to elude me during
the course of my research. Rich beamed when he realized that he
added a hitherto-unknown work to my endeavor and added glee-
fully, "You'll love the tagline: First he nails you … Then he nails
you!"

While I thanked Rich for his input, I realized that his offering
epitomized the greatest problem in creating a book of this nature.
On the one hand, there was an extraordinary quantity of Jesus-
centric and Jesus-inspired films to be explored. On the other hand,
the subject was too vast and unwieldy, with a surplus of titles that
are unfamiliar to most audiences – and, perhaps, rightfully so.

If an inventory were to be compiled of every film with a Jesus
element to it – even one as unlikely as *Jesus Christ: Serial Rapist* – it
would take more than a single book to do the encyclopedic justice
to the subject. As a result, I determined that tight parameters would
need to be set up around this project.

The primary concern that I needed to address was the question
of quantity. I decided that this book would limit its attention to
Jesus-centric films created for theatrical exhibition and film festivals. As a result, this guideline would exclude works that were created for television, the nontheatrical market aimed at exclusively for
screenings in churches and schools and the direct-to-video scene
– mercifully, *Jesus Christ: Serial Rapist* falls into the latter category
and I can promise that will be the very last time you'll hear that title

in these pages. Also absent are films made for viewing in the virtual reality format, such as *Jesus VR – The Story of Christ* (2016) and *7 Miracles* (2018).

Keeping the core of the book on theatrical releases will omit many fine works from discussion, most notably the groundbreaking 1953 U.S. television film *I Beheld His Glory*, Roberto Rossellini's sublime 1975 Italian television production *Il Messia*, and Franco Zeffirelli's acclaimed 1977 mini-series *Jesus of Nazareth*. Admittedly, it is a difficult sacrifice to make, but I believe this level of streamlining is necessary to keep a tight focus on how audiences viewed Jesus on the big screen.

Furthermore, the book will keep the spotlight on films about the life of Jesus or featuring the adult Jesus as a key character in the story. This will disqualify films involving individuals who believe they are the reincarnation of Christ or behave in a Christ-like manner, including two highly regarded works from 1957 (Carl Theodor Dreyer's *Ordet* and Jules Dassin's *He Who Must Die*), a pair of wacky comedies from 1972 (Robert Downey Sr.'s *Greaser's Palace* and Peter Medak's *The Ruling Class*) and Denys Arcand's 1989 Academy Award-nominated *Jesus of Montreal*. The sole exception to this rule is *Parable*, a short film that created controversy when it was screened at the 1964/65 World's Fair in New York; due to the historic precedent that *Parable* created in the cinematic depiction of Jesus' life, its place in the development of Jesus-centric cinema needs to be explored.

Also absent from in-depth consideration are films that focus exclusively on the birth of Jesus, including the 1912 (and partially lost) silent film *The Star of Bethlehem*, Iranian filmmaker Shahriar Bahrani's 2000 production *Saint Mary*, Catherine Hardwick's 2006 *The Nativity Story* and the 2017 animated feature *The Star*. An exception to this rule is Jean-Luc Godard's *Hail Mary*, but this will only receive a brief citation due to its papal condemnation (a rarity for this genre) and its appearance during a time when Jesus-centric films were becoming controversial. While it is a shame to leave Nativity-inspired works on the sidelines, this book is focused strictly on the cinematic interpretation of the adult Jesus.

In compiling this book, a dedicated effort was made to encompass films from all corners of the global cinema market. This was not an easy goal to meet, as many Jesus-centric films from Latin America, the Middle East, Africa and Asia have not been widely seen outside of their native countries and are not easily accessible to most filmgoers in the West. I will offer my apologies in advance if any worthwhile productions from around the world were either omitted or were not given the depth and scope of consideration offered to comparable works from the U.S. and Western European film industries.

Also, a large number of silent films on the subject cannot be seen today either because no prints are known to survive or because the extant materials are not readily available for screening; a notorious Jesus-inspired pornographic film from the 1970s is also considered lost. I have relied on historical documentation to cover the void created by these absent works, with the hope that complete copies will be available for appraisal in the future.

Finally, the writing of this book concluded in December 2020 while several Jesus-centric films – most notably the Terrence Malick production that was initially called *The Last Planet* and later renamed *The Way of the Wind*, with Hungarian actor Géza Röhrig as Jesus – were still in either pre-production or post-production. Hopefully, the opportunity will arise to update this book with future editions highlighting works that gained release after this version was published.

Foreword: A Uniquely Spiritual Art Form

By Rev. Caleb Scott Evans

"In the beginning was the Word, and the Word was with God, and the Word was God."
—John 1:1

Faith and film are closely associated in my memory and in my experience. While I love cinema, this love is not the result of fond childhood memories. I became a film lover in adulthood, but at a time that was exceptionally formative for me. I became a film lover while I was studying in seminary, preparing to become a Christian pastor.

The process of coming to love cinema happened so organically that it is difficult to pinpoint exactly when it happened. One pivotal moment happened when I stumbled upon the film *Solaris* by the great Russian director Andrei Tarkovsky. The film happened to be available on a streaming service I was using at the time. Tarkovsky is, unfortunately and unfairly, known as a 'difficult' director, but I had no awareness of that reputation at the time. Instead, I found myself hypnotized by the long and slow-paced film. It was not boring. It was contemplative, full of poetic imagery, and unafraid to deal with spiritual and deeply human themes.

From there, I came to realize that film could be a uniquely spiritual art form. I jumped into my newfound appreciation for film with both feet, spending my days in class studying Christian theology, and spending my free time exploring the cinematic landscape. Faith and film became closely associated in my mind. I viewed film, as I do all of life, through the lens of my Christian faith, and I came to appreciate film on a spiritual level.

As an undergraduate, I had majored in literature, and had found much of modern and postmodern literature unappealing. It was not that I was opposed to innovative works of art. No, my complaint with much of modern and postmodern literature was that it did not take spiritual themes seriously.

The same cannot be said of film, which came into its own as an art form in the modern era. The great directors were unafraid to explore spiritual themes and questions of faith to a far greater extent, in my reckoning, than many of the great writers who worked in the same period. Part of that difference may be due to the unique characteristics of film. Film, I believe, is uniquely suited to explore spiritual things. It is able to stage grand recreations of biblical events. It is able to depict the passage of time, right before our eyes. It is able to help us visualize the internal lives of human beings. It is able to give us a sense of eternity. It is able to portray truth, beauty, and goodness in a way that impacts us immediately. It is difficult to delve too deeply into cinema without spiritual questions being raised.

Some great films have been, in effect, devotional works. They were created with faith as their primary inspiration. On the other hand, there are great films which view faith with skepticism, while still treating spiritual concerns as being of vital importance. The films of the great Swedish director Ingmar Bergman, who identified as agnostic, come to mind. Looking at his work, it is hard not to see his films as, in a sense, God-haunted. In Bergman's films, God's perceived silence or absence is treated as a thing of utmost importance, and the impact of God's perceived silence, in those films, is frequently nightmarish. In so many great cinematic works of art, God is of central importance, even when the artists involved were and are not, themselves, religious believers. In essence, I believe that we see the impact of humanity's innate longing for the presence of God all over the history of film.

There is something transcendent about film, something about its ability to depict human beings moving through time and space, even long after those people are gone. There is something transcendent about the ability of cinema to merge the impermanent with the eternal. That being the case, I do not find it at all surprising that Jesus is a recurring figure in cinematic history.

Christians believe that Jesus is the incarnate Son of God. We believe that the eternal God entered into human history, became a human being, lived and died, and conquered death. As we look at the human condition, we see that human beings are faced with a sense that time and mortality are stalking us. We can see a glimpse of this concern in the plots of most films. Time moves forward. The plot races on to almost-certain disaster. There is a specter of fear and loss hanging around in the background.

Christians believe that the disaster, the loss, that we might have expected, when we look at our lives and when we look at human existence, has been forever altered because God took on our humanity, entered into time, and entered into suffering and death, which are a universal part of our human existence. We believe that God redeemed us from death, to raise mortal human beings to eternal life.

As I write this foreword in early January of 2021, we have recently celebrated Christmas, and I am reminded of what the theologian Hans Urs von Balthasar once wrote: "Christmas is not an event within history but is rather the invasion of time by eternity." I would amend this idea slightly to propose that Christmas, God becoming man, is the invasion of time by eternity precisely because it is an event within history.

How are these theological musings relevant to the history of portrayals of Jesus in film? I would put it this way: Spiritual cinema, at its best, offers us a glimpse of the invasion of time by eternity. I believe that film can be an important medium for prompting people to think about spiritual questions: Questions about time, eternity, mortality, and transcendence. It can prompt people to consider the questions of who God is and what our existence means. It can prompt people to consider who Jesus is.

As I think about Jesus, I am reminded of something that the great Russian author Fyodor Dostoevsky once wrote in a letter. He said this about Jesus: "I believe that there is nothing lovelier, deeper, more sympathetic, more rational, more manly, and more perfect than the Savior; I say to myself with jealous love that not only is there no one else like Him, but that there could be no one."

I believe that, not only is this statement about Jesus true, but also that cinematic art carries great potential to bear witness to this reality.

Rev. Caleb Scott Evans is the minister of Holy Trinity Anglican Church in Plainville, Connecticut.

Chapter One: In the Beginning of Cinema, There Was Jesus

"The Lord will fight for you, and you have only to be silent."
– Exodus 14:14

When the motion picture industry began to take shape in the 1890s, many of the earliest productions were about Jesus Christ. However, His presence in the most secular of popular entertainment formats is rarely acknowledged, even by the most learned of cinema scholars.

The failure to point out the influence of the Gospels on the pioneering filmmakers cannot be blamed on an anti-Christian conspiracy. Rather, it can be attributed to the longstanding absence of these films from the cinematic knowledge base. The 1897 films *La Passion du Christ* by the French filmmaker Albert Kirchner and a filmed record of *The Horitz Passion Play*, a Bohemian-based theatrical presentation, were the earliest known examples of Jesus-centric cinema, but prints of both productions became lost many years ago.

Also missing are two early works by pioneers in filmmaking: the 1898 *The Passion Play* by the American producer Siegmund Lubin and the 1899 *Christ Walking on Water* by the French filmmaker Georges Méliès. Perhaps the most ambitious Jesus-centric film project of the late 1890s was created in Australia by the Salvation Army's Limelight Department, which was also one of the world's first movie studios. This endeavor involved the creation of 13 films running approximately 90 seconds each that told the story of Jesus' ministry. The films were shot in 1899 and blended together in 1900 into *Soldiers of the Cross*, a presentation that also involved photographic glass slides that illustrated Jesus' experience along with live music and commentary by Herbert Booth, a Salvation Army officer responsible for the Limelight Department's contents. This could be considered to be the first known example of a multimedia presentation. Sadly, none of the films from *Soldiers of the Cross* have survived.

Frank Russell as Jesus in a surviving fragment from The Passion Play of Oberammergau *(1898).*

The oldest extant Jesus-centric film is the French 1898 production *La vie et la passion de Jésus-Christ* (*The Life and Passion of Jesus Christ*) by George Hatot and the Lumière Brothers. By contemporary standards, the film is gruelingly primitive. But if we put ourselves in the mind frame of audiences at the tail-end of the 19th century, the production is astonishing.

In this work, Jesus is already born in a manger with unusually high ceilings and a cow as the only non-human witness to the Nativity. The shadows cast on the back wall from the actors suggest the film was shot in natural light. A shepherd admires the infant, and the Three Wise Men come parading in to genuflect and present their gifts before the newborn.

Mary and Joseph are next seen in Egypt. A large and none-too-accurate drawing of the Sphinx is behind them, and there is a convenient ladder at the base of the massive sculpture. Mary takes the infant Jesus and climbs the ladder to seek rest within the paws of the Sphinx. A phalanx of centurions abruptly rushes in, but stop to raise their arms and bow at the mother and child resting at the Sphinx while Joseph and his donkey look on dumbfounded.

The scene shifts to a painted backdrop of what appears to be a garden. A body covered in a white blanket is brought out by two men and laid on a stone while a woman in black weeps. The adult Jesus appears and is briefed on the matter. Jesus extends His arms and then points skyward, at which point the man under the blanket sits up, shocking everyone witnessing the incident.

The scene cuts to what could be a room in a palace – there are rich-looking curtains hanging on the walls. Centurions open the curtains and a nobleman in a toga walks in. A shifty-looking man is brought in and, after the briefest of exchanges, he is given a box before exiting. The man in the toga stares at the curtains for a few extra seconds.

Next is the Last Supper, where Jesus is kissed by His Disciples before the food is served. A brief blackout brings us to Gethsemane, where the trees look oddly like large undersea coral. The shifty-looking man and the aristocrat in the toga show up with centurions, who arrest Jesus. Then, we're back at the palace where the shifty-looking man appears briefly before the toga-clad aristocrat and departs before the arrested Jesus shows up. A woman and two men plead for mercy, but a man in black starts whipping Jesus in gentle slow-motion strokes. Then we are back in Gethsemane, where a centurion puts the crown of thorns on Jesus' head. Two centurions arrive with the cross, which Jesus carries off-screen. Calvary is positioned in front of a wall, where Jesus and the two thieves show little signs of agony while on their crosses. Jesus' tomb is a marble coffin sitting before the same wall where He was crucified. His body is laid to rest, but no sooner is the coffin lid sealed than Jesus pushes it away and arises from the dead.

Admittedly, the task of telescoping the life of Jesus into ten minutes requires heavy editing, although the mixed-up Passion – with Caiaphas and Pilate conflated and Jesus being condemned to carry His cross from Gethsemane – must have confused some people watching this for the first time in 1898. Still, the effort was admirable for the rough work-in-progress filmmaking period.

Now, let's jump across the Atlantic to see what the American cinema pioneers were attempting. In 1897, Thomas Edison received a patent for a device called the Kinetograph, which used celluloid film to create moving pictures. Edison was zealous in protecting his patent – he was aware of the commercial potential that existed in the creation and exhibition of this new medium, and he was eager to create a monopolistic control before it could expand into a full-blown industry.

Still, the clever minds of the day were not easily frightened by the complexity of Edison's patented creation or his well-known penchant for bringing litigation against potential rivals. One of those who sought to challenge Edison was a resourceful Englishman named William C. Paley, who happily circumvented Edison's control and created his own motion picture camera.

In circumstances that are not quite clear today, Paley hooked up with fellow Englishman Richard G. Hollaman, who ran a hodge-podge New York venue called Eden Musee that specialized in waxwork exhibits, marionette shows, magic lantern shows, and the new motion picture presentations. In the summer of 1897, Hollaman entered into an informal agreement with W.B. Hurd, who was headed to Europe to film the staging of a Passion Play in Bohemia.

Hurd initially agreed to premiere the footage of this filmed record at the Eden Musee, but reneged on his deal with Hollaman and sold the rights to the theatrical production company Klaw & Erlanger, which packaged the work as *The Horitz Passion Play* (named for the village where this dramatic presentation of the final days of Jesus' life was staged). Hurd's footage was presented in Philadelphia in 1897, with Hollaman in attendance. However, Hollaman was not impressed with the Hurd footage from Europe and believed that he could create something better using the same material.

Hollaman recalled a failed 1880 theatrical version of the Passion Play penned by Salmi Morse and discovered the rights to the work belonged to a costume company owned by Albert Eaves, who was a friend of Frank Russell, an actor and a Hollaman acquaintance. Hollaman conspired with Eaves and Russell to create their own version of the Passion Play – and in a groundbreaking work of cinematic fraudulence, they would claim it was a recorded version of the famous Passion Play presented in the German village of Oberammergau – even though much of Morse's text deviated considerably from the celebrated German work.

This unlikely endeavor corralled William C. Paley, who not only had his own movie camera but also created a projector called the Kalatechnoscope that could project the film on a screen. Theatrical director Henry C. Vincent was hired, with Frank Russell cast in the key role of Jesus. A studio was set up on the roof of the Grand Central Palace, a 13-story New York City exhibition hall, to accommodate the production.

From the beginning of production, things went awry. Overhead studio lights had yet to be invented, so filming relied entirely on whatever available sunlight beamed across the Grand Central Palace rooftop. Vincent had no concept of how to shoot a film, but since he was contractually tied to the production he could not be easily fired. Thus, he was carefully shooed off the set by Russell and Paley with the fib that they could not shoot any scenes due to insufficient light – and once Vincent was gone, Russell and Paley took over the day's work. Under these circumstances, it took six weeks to shoot 23 scenes totaling approximately 2,000 feet of film. Paley's camera captured the production at a 30 frames per second speed – when projected, this totaled 20 minutes of screen action.

The finished work was titled *The Passion Play of Oberammergau* and Hollaman commissioned a poster to advertise the work – the first known example of a film poster. *The Passion Play of Oberammergau* premiered on January 30, 1898 at Eden Musee. Because the concept of intertitles was not yet invented, the film was shown with an off-screen narrator detailing the various scenes.

Even though the medium was brand new, it was immediately clear to audiences of the era that *The Passion Play of Oberammergau* was not filmed in Germany. The *New York Herald* denounced the fraud, stating: "All the preliminary announcements of this exhibition have tended to convey the impression that this is a genuine reproduction of the celebrated passion play at Oberammergau." Klaw & Erlanger tried to halt the screenings of Hollaman's work, but this only added to the publicity for the presentation.

Despite the chicanery of the marketing, *The Passion Play of Oberammergau* was praised by New York-area clergy who attended screenings. Hollaman began to receive requests for screenings outside of New York, and he started to sell prints for a then-exorbitant fee of $850 per copy.

At this point, Thomas Edison pounced. Claiming Paley violated his patent for the motion picture camera, Edison took Hollaman and his creative collaborators to court – and won. Hollaman was required to turn over the negative and the rights to *The Passion Play of Oberammergau.*

Alas, Edison's court victory spelled the defeat of this pioneering film production. Edison broke the complete 20-minute film into segments that were sold separately to exhibitors, although the complete production was still being shown as late as December 1899.

Edison's control on the nascent film industry by citing his patent on the film camera came to an end in 1902, when the U.S. Court of Appeals ruled that Edison only owned rights to the sprocket system that moved perforated film through the camera and not the complete concept of the motion picture camera. By that time, however, it was too late for Hollaman to retrieve the rights to *The Passion Play of Oberammergau.* The damage was already done.

Today, *The Passion Play of Oberammergau* only exists in a fragment that is preserved at the George Eastman House in Rochester, New York; no copies of the 20-minute version are known to survive. Hollaman and his collaborators slipped into obscurity, quickly forgotten by a film industry they had helped to launch. And, as mentioned earlier, *The Horitz Passion Play* that inspired the creation of Hollman's work no longer exists.

One might think that the hoax pulled by Hollaman and his comrades would have taught the early film industry a lesson about being honest. It didn't, although the shaky behavior shifted from passing off fraudulent presentations to stealing other people's works.

In the early years of the 20th century, the motion picture industry was plagued with incessant bootlegging of films. Shady characters who passed themselves off as producers and distributors would obtain copies of films and claim it as their own property, selling prints to unsuspecting exhibitors that were unaware of the original source material. This was particularly problematic with European filmmakers who did not have a U.S. sales presence and, thus, could not defend their property outside of their continent.

Legal enforcement of cinematic intellectual property was still in its infancy at that time, so the threat of litigation was not the best strategy. The French company Pathé Frères came up with an odd yet effective solution when it was preparing the release of its 1903 production *La vie et la passion de Jésus Christ*: the company's logo was a rooster, and everyone involved in the film industry was aware of that symbol. Even audiences recognized the poultry logo. But rather than limiting the rooster logo to the opening credits, Pathé Frères made it part of the Biblical epic.

In watching *La vie et la passion de Jésus Christ* today, it is difficult not to fall into the habit of playing "spot the rooster" as the symbolic fowl was stenciled on the walls and stairwells of many of the film's scenes; it is also on the side of the Disciples' boat when they view Jesus walking on water. Strangely, it is absent from the scene of Peter denying Jesus after the rooster crows three times.

None of the characters in the film called attention to the presence of a rooster stencil that shadowed Jesus as He traveled across the Holy Land, and one can assume that most of the audiences in 1903 weren't wondering about why an illustrated rooster kept turning up in ancient Judea. However, the ubiquity of this symbol helped to keep *La vie et la passion de Jésus Christ* from being bootlegged endlessly – and for a number of years, other filmmakers borrowed this trick of sticking logos into the scenes.

But what about the film that Pathé Frères was trying to protect? *La vie et la passion de Jésus Christ* was an unusual production for its time. Back when most films were only one-reel in length and produced on modest budgets, *La vie et la passion de Jésus Christ* spanned a rather epic 44 minutes and was presented with a large cast and extravagant production design, including an extensive hand-stenciling of scenes to achieve color cinematography effects.

La vie et la passion de Jésus Christ breaks the story of Jesus into vignettes that are introduced by title cards heralding the event to be depicted. There are no intertitle dialogue breaks – which is understandable, as the story would have been extremely familiar to most audiences at the time and intertitles would have disrupted the pageant depictions.

La vie et la passion de Jésus Christ incorporates special effects throughout its presentation, starting with the Annunciation and the appearance of an angel standing on a cloud and followed by the appearance of the Star of Bethlehem above the shepherds. The double exposure style of the camera trickery calls to mind the charming cinematic magic of Georges Méliès, albeit with a more pronounced seriousness instead of Méliès' feats of happy tomfoolery.

The film finds Mary and Joseph walking into Bethlehem in search of a place to stay; later New Testament films would have the pregnant Mary riding a donkey rather than traveling on foot. There is an unintentionally funny scene when the Wise Men and the shepherds crowd into the already-cramped manger to view the newborn Jesus – the presence of so many people in a tiny space recalls the classic stateroom scene from the Marx Brothers' *A Night at the Opera*, albeit without the slapstick blackout gag.

The film also oomphs up the story by adding a group of musically gifted angels to play for the infant Jesus as He rests in His crib. When Mary and Joseph flee into Egypt, the audience knows where they are because the Holy Family rests with the Sphinx and the pyramids behind them.

Obviously, the entire life of Jesus could not be telescoped into the 44-minute running time, so Jesus' adult life is truncated. The grown-up Jesus encounters John the Baptist and then turns water into wine at Cana before Mary Magdalene shows up to clean His feet. A visually impressive (although somewhat eccentric) depiction of Jesus walking on water finds Him ascending from the depths of a churning sea and walking casually with outstretched arms while the waves crash around him. A brief consideration of the Transfiguration is depicted with Jesus conversing casually with Moses and Elijah.

Nearly all of *La vie et la passion de Jésus Christ* is shot with a static camera positioned far from the actors, as if a stage play is being recorded. There are two brief cutaway scenes: Jesus accepting his Pilate-dictated fate with the words "Ecce Homo" on a wall behind him and the apocryphal Veronica holding up the cloth that captured Jesus' image after she wiped his face during his trek to Golgotha. (The presence of Veronica and the cloth with Jesus' image is not part of the canonical Gospels, but with this film it became a staple of Jesus-centric cinema for years to come.)

La vie et la passion de Jésus Christ also offers a whimsical consideration of the Resurrection, with angels carefully lifting the tomb and Jesus' ghostly spirit rising up and floating around, frightening away the centurions guarding His resting place. In the Ascension, Jesus rides a circular cloud into Heaven, where he sits next to God (a white-haired man with a flowing white beard) and begins to converse with the same casual nature that defined the film's depiction of the Transfiguration.

The direction of *La vie et la passion de Jésus Christ* is credited to Ferdinand Zecca and Lucien Nonguet. There is no record of the actors in the cast – the performer in the role of Jesus appears to be a bit on the hefty side, a considerable difference from the more svelte actors that would play this role later on. Most of the film was shot on painted sets, with only a few exterior shots, notably the rocky tomb that held Lazarus.

La vie et la passion de Jésus Christ was an extremely popular film on both sides of the Atlantic and, remarkably, it was still enjoying theatrical playdates as late as 1932, well into the sound-film era.

Apparently, the Pathé Frères film was also very popular with Gaumont Film Company, a rival French studio. Alice Guy, Gaumont's head of production, as well as the first female director in the motion picture history, seemed to have studied *La vie et la passion de Jésus Christ* with extraordinary precision, as her 1906 film *La vie du Jesus* bears more than a passing resemblance to the Zecca-Nonguet collaboration.

La vie du Jesus follows the same structure as *La vie et la passion de Jésus Christ*, with title cards announcing scenes from Jesus' life that are presented in pageant format without intertitle interruptions. Even some of the more pronounced eccentricities of *La vie et la passion de Jésus Christ* – the arrival of Joseph and Mary on foot in Bethlehem, the overflowing crowd arriving at the manger, the angels playing musical instruments over the sleeping infant Jesus, the cutaway to Veronica displaying Jesus' image on the sweat-wiped cloth, the angels lifting the tomb lid while the resurrected Jesus floats skyward – are duplicated in Guy's work.

But running roughly 33 minutes, Guy's work is shorter than *La vie et la passion de Jésus Christ* and, thus, critical aspects of Jesus' life are omitted: John the Baptist is nowhere to be seen and Jesus' walking on water is absent. Guy's depiction of Jesus' adult ministry prior to the entry into Jerusalem is limited to the encounter with the Samaritan woman at the well, the raising of Jairus' daughter and Mary Magdalene washing Jesus' feet – all of these were also included in the 1903 film.

Where Guy's film differs from the Zecca-Nonguet film is the use of exteriors for the Gethsemane and road to Calvary scenes, although it doesn't help that the same forest clearing was used for both segments. Guy's film also includes some brief and middling camera panning, although this effect is not used with any great dramatic value.

Unlike *La vie et la passion de Jésus Christ*, *La vie du Jesus* did not have a lengthy theatrical life. Many of Guy's films became lost over time and for many years *La vie du Jesus* was among her missing works. The film's eventual recovery was cited by film scholars in the belated appreciation of Guy's contribution to the development of cinematic art.

But perhaps some film scholars invested too much importance into *La vie du Jesus*, owing to the director's pioneering role as a female filmmaker. For example, consider the lavish praise from historian Gwendolyn Audrey Foster in the September 2013 edition of *Film International*.

"In *La vie du Christ*, women are foregrounded as central characters and witnesses to the spectacle of Christ's birth," Foster wrote. "Christ himself is feminized and eroticized. In general, performances are unlike those of other films of the same period. Characters are suffused with familiarity, carnality and corporeality. Sets combine highly artificial indoor *tableaux vivantes* with outdoor scenes and neorealist staging … In this departure from recognized classics of the period, Guy refigures the performance of gender in the Christ parable, emphasizing and privileging women and children as active participants who perform in a spectacle that combines theatricality with an almost neorealist and decidedly feminist vision."

Perhaps Foster is speaking more about her hopes for what the Guy film could have been rather than the production itself. The distance between the camera and the performers prevents any degree of intimacy, while the theatricality of the film acting was typical of the first decade of the 20th century. And Foster's assertion regarding the presence of a "feminized and eroticized" Jesus is very much a minority opinion.

Likewise, David Shepherd, Assistant Professor in Hebrew Bible/Old Testament and Director, Trinity Centre for Biblical Studies at Dublin's Trinity College, credits Guy's imagery on her purchase of a copy of Jacques Tissot's *Illustrated Bible* in 1900 rather than the Zecca-Nonguet film. Shepherd also tries to invest proto-feminist politics into Guy's work, especially where it was clearly not intended.

"In the scene of the nativity and the visit of the magi, Guy introduces a feminine presence in the shape of two women within the retinue of the Magi, who come and bow to the infant Jesus and then take up positions nearest the manger itself—precisely where Guy and the audience would expect any maternally minded women to locate themselves," Shepherd proclaimed. "That two women are given pride of place within the composition of the scene and are moreover allowed to visibly participate in the adoration alongside the Magi is our first hint that Guy's concern and maternal interest will extend far beyond Mary."

But the Zecca-Nonuet film also included women and girls in the manger scene, including a clearly visible Black woman at a time when multicultural casting was unknown. The Zecca-Nonuet film also includes a sequence on the Massacre of the Innocents, with the women of Bethlehem bravely attempting to shield their infants while physically beating back the assault of the homicidal centurions. An argument could be made that the "concern and maternal interest" Shepherd saw in Guy's film was far more obvious in the earlier production.

This criticism should not be construed as a belittling of Guy's historic importance – her value as a creative artist was not widely appreciated during her career, and it is understandable for scholars to make a corybantic effort in rescuing her from obscurity. But the truth remains that *La vie et la passion de Jésus Christ* made a greater impact in its day than *La vie du Jesus* – and, quite frankly, the earlier work is a more satisfying experience. Still, both productions represented important steps forward in the development of films focused on Biblical themes.

Jesus in Feature-Length Films

A major step forward in both the genre of Jesus-focused cinema and in the American film industry was the 1912 feature *From the Manger to the Cross*. Up until this film's production, any cinematic consideration of the life of Jesus was created within the confines of the studio. This work moved far from the confines of a studio to location shooting in Palestine (then part of the Ottoman Empire) and Egypt. Thus, all New Testament films shot on far-flung locations owe a debt to this 1912 endeavor.

Ironically, the film came about almost by accident. The Kalem Company, a studio founded in 1907, had no problems with sending film crews to work in distant locations if they could secure geographically appropriate exterior shots. Kalem's ace director Sidney Olcott, along with his screenwriter and leading lady Gene Gauntier, took a camera crew to Europe in 1910, shooting films on locations in Germany and Ireland. These works were popular with American audiences, many of whom were European immigrants happy to see their homelands again, this time on the big screen.

In 1912, Kalem approved their travel to North Africa and the Middle East, with the plan of shooting travelogues and short films with exotic locations. While in Egypt, Gauntier was stricken with heatstroke. During her recovery, she wondered if it would be possible to shoot a feature film based on the life of Jesus at the historic sites mentioned in the Gospels. With Kalem's approval, Olcott and Gauntier reached out for British theater actor Robert Henderson-Bland to travel to the Holy Land to portray Jesus in their film, which Olcott directed and Gauntier wrote and co-starred in as the Virgin Mary.

As its title would suggest, *From the Manger to the Cross* traces Jesus' life from the Annunciation through the Crucifixion. The film takes full advantage of its historic locations to recreate passages of Jesus' life within Middle Eastern environment, most dramatically with the Flight into Egypt, where Mary and Joseph pause from their self-exile in the shadow of the Sphinx and the Pyramids.

Olcott and Gauntier were creating their film on the cheap, which prevented them from staging the massive sequences that audiences would later expect from on-location Biblical films. Likewise, the presence of the angels in the Annunciation and Nativity sequences is only hinted at, with the actors looking skyward for entities that are not visible to the audience. While shooting in the Holy Land, Olcott and Gauntier corralled rural villagers to serve as extras, and the infant Jesus was played by the baby of a Western couple traveling through the region. But the presence of the production was not always welcomed – at one point, Olcott and Gauntier found their lives were in danger when Arab locals in Jerusalem objected to the presence of Westerners filming a Christian movie in their ancient city.

Olcott and Gauntier were also at a disadvantage with the silent film medium when it came to relating Jesus' parables and teachings.

Although the intertitles were taken from New Testament passages, the filmmakers considered it unfeasible to print out the entire Biblical passages as intertitles. As a result, *From the Manger to the Cross* omits the bulk of Jesus' parables and teachings and puts more emphasis on the miracles that He performed in His lifetime. For example, the miracle of the Wedding at Cana is presented with a flash of light directly into Jesus' face as He pronounces the changing of the water into wine. Throughout the film, wretched people (including Olcott doing double-duty playing a blind man) run their fingers along Jesus' cloak and suddenly begin shooting their arms into air to proclaim their abrupt arrival in perfect health. Jesus' walking on the water was created back at the Kalem Studios via a somewhat obvious use of double exposure trick-photography.

As a director, Olcott was both imaginative and limited. Film historian Daniel Eagan, writing in his book *America's Film Legacy*, wisely observed that Olcott "composed frames with strong diagonals that pulled viewers to specific areas in the foreground or background, and moved his actors in arcs that carried them first towards and then away from the camera, depending on the requirements of the scene." Eagan also praised cinematographer George Hollister for his camera panning, which was not common in 1912, and his ability to capture vibrant imagery using harsh exterior lighting and a limited amount of film stock.

But Olcott was also bound by much of the protocol of that era's filmmaking. Despite the aforementioned camera panning, the bulk of the film was shot from a stagnant viewpoint, which captured much on-screen commotion without any camera motion. Also, much of the acting seemed to be framed for the theatrical proscenium rather than the big screen – Robert Henderson-Bland's Jesus was frequently problematic, with grand emoting and melodramatic hand gestures that (to today's viewers) seems like an overdone pantomime.

And still, *From the Manger to the Cross* offers a great deal of wonderment that has not grown stale. The depiction of the Nativity is particularly moving, when the shepherds enter the manger and stand around Mary and the infant Jesus, peering at the newborn with utter astonishment. This is followed with the Three Wise Men describing their mission to a visibly agitated Herod (played by George Kellogg, a stage actor, in his only known film role). Robert G. Vignola's Judas is also notable, capturing both the sense of villainous mischief and a gnawing realization that nothing good will come from his actions.

From the Manger to the Cross was first screened for clergy in London and New York in late 1912 before being made available to the general public in 1913. The film was a major commercial hit, and when Kalem went out of business in 1917, the rights were sold to Vitagraph. The film was still playing in theatrical release as late as 1938, and in 1998 it became the first film based on the New Testament to be added to the Library of Congress' National Film Registry.

From the Manger to the Cross ran for five reels in its initial release and clocked in at one hour and eleven minutes for its re-release in the late 1930s; some re-released versions included a burial and resurrection segment featuring a different actor playing Jesus. And while *From the Manger to the Cross* was not the first feature-length film, it helped to push religious-themed filmmaking away from short-length works to more lengthy productions.

In 1913, one year after *From the Manger to the Cross* debuted, *The Shadow of Nazareth* appeared, offering an invented narrative concerning the love triangle between Barabbas, Judith Iscariot (the hitherto unheralded sister of Judas) and Caiaphas. This leads to melodramatic anguish that results in Barabbas getting arrested by Caiaphas' machinations, followed by the Sanhedrin leader convincing Judas to betray Jesus. After Jesus is condemned, Barabbas is freed from prison, Judas hangs himself and Judith stabs Caiaphas to death before committing suicide.

Perhaps unknown to the makers of *The Shadow of Nazareth*, Italian filmmakers had their own retelling the life of Judas in 1911 with *Giuda*, which tried to explain Judas' betrayal. The film blames Judas' treachery on the influence of another literary creation – in this case, Priscilla, a courtesan who failed to entice Jesus and then manipulated the weak-willed Judas to enact her revenge.

But the Italian cinema took a bold step forward in 1913 with the groundbreaking production of Henryk Sienkiewicz's novel *Quo*

Vadis? Rather that settle for a modest two-reeler, this work was released in a two-hour edition, setting a new standard in cinematic presentation. Produced by Società Italiana Cines on a then-record budget of $150,000, *Quo Vadis?* was a full-fledged spectacle complete with scores of costumed extras, three-dimensional sets (not the painted backdrops used in most films of the era), and elaborate sequences, including a quasi-orgy for the Emperor Nero and a climax that featured racing chariots and lions attacking Christian martyrs in Rome's Colosseum.

Viewed today, *Quo Vadis?* is still a highly impressive work. The presence of dozens of centurions, the toga-clad Roman elite, scantily-clad "Syrian dancers" and armored gladiators provided the foundation for the modern movie epic. In moving away from the theatricality that anchored so much of the early silent movies, director Enrico Guazzoni wisely chose to shoot exterior scenes that showed the scope of the Roman countryside. This gave a rich degree of reality to scenes that required massive crowd action (particularly the panicked exodus during the burning of Rome), while sensitive moments such as the vision of Jesus to St. Peter on the outskirts of the city resonated, in large part, by having them placed in natural settings rather than in a studio.

In terms of religious piety, however, *Quo Vadis?* was not interested in playing up the Christian doctrines. The vision of Jesus comes near the very end of the film, with the somewhat eerie image of Jesus standing before a large glowing cross and casually breaking the chains of enslaved men.

Nonetheless, the film created a sensation when it crossed the Atlantic and opened in April 1913 at New York's Astor Theatre (a major Broadway house reconfigured as a cinema). The Astor charged an unprecedented $1.50 per ticket, but demand was so strong that the film played for nine months. Road show presentations took *Quo Vadis?* to other major cities, where the film inspired awe from audiences. The news of the American release helped to secure a special royal screening in London for King George V and Queen Mary.

The film also provoked other filmmakers to dream of making bigger films. An unlikely individual eager to use the power of film to proselytize was Charles Taze Russell, founder of the Jehovah's Witness movement. In 1914, Russell released *The Photo-Drama of Creation*, an eight-hour marathon work spanning four parts and incorporating films and photographic slides with synchronized sound in a mammoth overview of the Old and New Testaments.

The Photo-Drama of Creation was shown across North America, Europe, Australia and New Zealand and reportedly reached 9 million people; this epic production still survives and can be viewed in its entirety on YouTube. Clearly intended as a work of religious sincerity rather than an expression of cinematic art (most of the film segments are stiff and stagey), *The Photo-Drama of Creation* is nonetheless impressive for its daringness to present a Biblical drama in such a grand scale. The footage of Jesus' ministry features hand-colored prints reminiscent of the color film experiments from the early 1900s, with bold patches of bright hues (mostly on the actors' skin and garments) that light up against monochromatic settings. This is most effective with Jesus' entrance into Jerusalem, as the color-illustrated actors cheer his arrival while the black-and-white sky background gives the impression of an impending storm.

Perhaps the most inspired creative artist eager to outdo *Quo Vadis?* was D.W. Griffith. From 1908 through 1913, Griffith directed hundreds of one-reel and two-reel films for Biograph – the exact number is uncertain, since Griffith did not receive on-screen credit for his work and many of the films are now considered lost.

Despite his prolific output and growing proficiency in the direction of films, Griffith was stifled at Biograph, which had no interest in creating expensive feature films. Furthermore, the Biograph executives saw their company as an entertainment outlet while Griffith was growing interested in using film as a tool to expound on his notions of social injustice.

Griffith left Biograph in 1913 to join the Mutual Film Corp., an independently-operated film production and distribution company. But, again, Griffith faced the same problem that he encountered at Biograph: an executive level unwillingness to devote time and money to creating epic American features. Within a year of joining Mutual, Griffith began work on the film that would change both his life and his industry.

Today, it is impossible to discuss Griffith's 1915 Civil War epic *The Birth of a Nation* without focusing on the blatant racism of Griffith's revisionist spin on history. We don't need to rehash the vices of this film in this text, but we should point out that Griffith brought Jesus awkwardly into this mix, closing his polarizing film with a symbolic scene of a large group of white people wearing Biblical clothing who find comfort beneath a superimposed vision of a rather hirsute Jesus. The intertitle for the sequence reads: "Dare we dream of a golden day when the bestial War shall rule no more. But instead – the gentle Prince in the Hall of Brotherly Love in the City of Peace."

While *The Birth of a Nation* was a colossal commercial success, Griffith was the subject of hostile commentary from many critics, educators and civil rights leaders because of his reckless rewriting of history. Baffled and angry at the outrage he created, Griffith sought to answer his critics with a new production of an even greater stylistic and substantive vision. The resulting work was the 1916 masterpiece *Intolerance*, which many critics consider to be the first apex of screen art.

Harping on his long-simmering obsession with social injustice, Griffith created an unorthodox epic that spanned the centuries to tell four interweaving stories from different eras that detailed man's cruelty to his fellow beings. To the casual observer, the stories barely seemed connected: the fall of Babylon, the Crucifixion of Jesus, the slaughter of the French Huguenots in the 1572 St. Bartholomew's Day Massacre and a modern tale of corrupt capitalists and hypocritical morality in urban America. Connecting the stories was an image of a woman (played by Lillian Gish) from an undetermined era rocking a cradle while observing an unseen infant.

What did it all mean? Even Griffith's financial backers were hard pressed to come up with a coherent explanation. Griffith explained this experimental storytelling technique in this manner: "The stories begin like four currents looked at from a hilltop. At first the four currents flow apart, slowly and quietly. But as they flow, they grow nearer and nearer together, and faster and faster, until in the end, in the last act, they mingle in one mighty river of expressed emotion."

Intolerance did not offer four equal stories. The Babylonian tale – which is best known thanks to its massive sets and extraordinary quantity of extras – and the modern story dominated the running time, with the French story trailing with significantly less footage. The Judean story was the briefest of the bunch, consisting of seven short segments totaling ten minutes and sprinkled haphazardly across the three-hour film.

The first installment of the Judean story occurs about seven minutes into *Intolerance*. Jesus is not present, which is curious since the intertitle announces His coming by stating: "Ancient Jerusalem, the golden city whose people have given us many of our highest ideals, and from the carpenter shop of Bethlehem, sent us the Man of Men, the greatest enemy of intolerance." The viewer encounters "certain hypocrites amongst the Pharisees" who conduct their prayers in public, forcing all human traffic to come to a halt. Griffith plays the segment for laughs, with a toothless elderly man pausing from munching on a piece of fruit and a boy carrying an oversized bundle, struggling to keep it off the ground as the Pharisee goes through an obnoxious display of his self-perceived holiness. This three-minute scene was inspired by Jesus' parable of publican and tax collector, particularly with the Pharisee's amazing declaration, "O Lord I thank thee that I am not like other men."

Around the 55-minute mark, the audience gets to see Jesus for the first time. The sequence is inspired by the Wedding at Cana, which Griffith stages in a slightly farcical manner as a serene Jesus helps the frantic wedding party when it is discovered that they ran out of wine. Griffith has a shadow of a cross obscuring Jesus when the miracle is performed, and Jesus is seen watching with pleasure as the wedding continues with the beloved drink. Griffith also opts to explain to viewers the value of the miracle with an intertitle that states: "Wine was deemed a fit offering to God; the drinking of it a part of the Jewish religion."

There is more wine to be found 10 minutes later, when a jolly Jesus is seen at the center of a banquet – although wine is being served, He graciously declines a cup but encourages the others to imbibe. From a contemporary viewpoint, it might seem strange that Griffith is placing so much emphasis on Jesus and wine. But back in 1916, the Temperance Movement was making great strides to bring about a national effort to ban all alcohol sales. This would ultimately result in the passage of the Eighteenth Amendment to the U.S. Constitution in 1919, which led to the era known as Prohibition. (The Twenty-First Amendment would be ratified in 1933 to void the chaos created by the Prohibition period.) From his perspective, Griffith may have envisioned those seeking Prohibition as being intolerant of those who enjoyed wine.

Mercifully, Griffith recalled that there was more to Jesus' ministry than drinking wine, and he offered up a dramatization of the woman accused of adultery. To his credit, Griffith did not misidentify the woman as Mary Magdalene, and the scene is presented with a genuine sincerity as Jesus appears to share the pain experienced by the humiliated woman.

Around the 85-minute mark, the image of Jesus gathering children around Him – inspired by Mark 10:14's "Suffer the little children"– is presented in a 15-second segment after a heart-wrenching scene in the modern story when a young mother has her infant torn from her arms by the vicious members of a phony social reform society.

Jesus appears later in the film in two scenes – one running 30 seconds, the other 10 seconds – where He carries His cross along the Via Dolorosa, and finally in a five-second view of the Crucifixion.

Why did Griffith give the Judean story so little space within the massive stretch of *Intolerance*? It appears that the Judean story originally occupied much more on-screen territory. Film historians Roy Kinnard and Tim Davis determined that representatives from the Jewish service organization B'nai B'rith got word that Griffith's film planned to place most of the blame for Jesus' prosecution and death on the Sanhedrin leaders rather than the Roman occupying force. After meeting with the B'nai B'rith team, Griffith removed the offending footage and destroyed it. But since *Intolerance* was already running far over budget and behind schedule, the director decided not to shoot new footage to expand the Judean story. Still, the absence of Pontius Pilate makes it clear that Griffith viewed the intolerant attitude of the Pharisees as being the driving force that led to the Crucifixion.

But despite its lack of screen time, the Judean story is blessed with Howard Gaye's remarkable presence as Jesus. In a film where it seems that every major character is on the verge of a nervous breakdown, Gaye's Jesus epitomizes serenity in the Cana segment and compassion in the retelling of the rescue of the adulteress. The scenes with Jesus carrying the cross are stunning for the physical and psychological anguish that Gaye channels – the actor essays a level of power within a relatively few seconds that is nothing short of stunning.

Griffith's *Intolerance* opened in 1916 to very mixed reviews and disappointing box office returns. While its importance in the development of the motion picture art form is universally recognized today, its approach to the life of Jesus has raised disappointment. Film historian Richard Walsh dismissed the Judean story as "little more than a garnish" to the film's other stories, curtly observing that "a 'dash' of Jesus immediately ennobles the film." Another film historian, Peter Malone, believed that Griffith's Jesus was "more thematic rather than the picture of a rounded character." And Matt Page, the British author of the *Bible Films Blog*, complained of an "ultra-selective portrayal of Jesus," adding his wonder that "despite the Judean story's short running time, it's surprising that it is given so much attention in the study of Jesus films."

In the same year that *Intolerance* was released, producer Thomas H. Ince unfurled his antiwar epic *Civilization*. Ince co-directed the film with Reginald Barker and Raymond B. West, and the triple teamwork created a lack of cohesive style – at some points, *Civilization* is stunning, while at others it is painfully unsubtle.

Set is a fictitious European kingdom called Wredpryd – the Teutonic military uniforms and belligerent Kaiser-inspired monarch makes it obvious which country it is supposed to represent – the story opens with a philosophical schism between a government eager for war against rival countries and a growing Christian-focused pacifist movement that views war as being antithetical to their faith. The pacifists are mostly women who have no say in government – the lone male parliamentarian who openly espouses pacifism is violently assaulted in the street by a crowd of war-supporters. To fuel the war machinery, the military violently recruits men and boys from the rural countryside and forces them onto bloody battlefields.

In the midst of this situation is Count Ferdinand, an aristocrat whose fiancée has joined the pacifist movement. The count has invented a new submarine and the King orders him to use it in an ongoing war. While out at sea in his submarine, the count receives orders to sink a passenger ship that is believed to be carrying military contraband. This is clearly intended to recall the 1915 sinking of the Lusitania, which was torpedoed by a German U-boat. The count envisions the innocent lives that he would destroy and disobeys the order. When the crew tries a mutiny to force the sinking of the ship, Ferdinand starts firing a revolver at the mutineers and somehow manages to blow up his submarine.

Incredibly, Ferdinand is the sole survivor of his wreckage and is found by his kingdom's navy. (Yes, this was a bit too convenient for the story.) He is taken to the King's palace, but his survival seems unlikely due to the changing political climate. At this point, the film goes off in a direction that was unprecedented for the cinema of that era: the count finds himself in a hellish purgatory where naked and forlorn souls writhe in pain and anguish. Into this setting comes Jesus, who laments to the count, "Many evils are being done in my name." Because Ferdinand opted to save the lives of the innocents on the passenger ship, Jesus informs him that he will not be condemned to Hell. (The fact that Ferdinand's actions caused the deaths of everyone on his submarine is casually overlooked.)

In the most remarkable moment of the film, Jesus temporarily vanishes and then returns to take possession of Ferdinand's body. With Jesus occupying his body, Ferdinand heals rapidly and quickly begins preaching a pacifist message – to the astonishment of the King and the military. The King has Ferdinand arrested and sentenced to death – a decision that brings out an army of mostly female pacifists who surround the palace.

The King then learns that Ferdinand died in his prison cell, thus avoiding execution by hanging. In the cell, the King experiences a vision of Jesus, who shows the monarch the suffering and misery brought by his war. Jesus also informs the King that his name is written within the Book of Judgment "on a page stained with the blood of your people." The King leaves the cell and agrees to sign an unconditional peace treaty. The kingdom rejoices as its warriors return to their families.

Created during the American period of isolationism prior to involvement in World War I, *Civilization* offers the blunt message that one cannot be a Christian and support a nation's involvement in war. The decision to take Jesus out of a New Testament setting and make him an integral character in a contemporary story was astonishing for the era and some critics in 1916 were unhappy with this plot device – most notably Henry Christeen Warnack in the *Los Angeles Times*, who sneered at the film as an "error in judgment" and worried that the inclusion of Jesus would be considered offensive to Christians.

The role of Jesus went to George Fisher, a relatively minor actor who never achieved top-tier stardom in the silent film era and failed to make the transition into sound films. Ahead of the film's release, Fisher told the *Los Angeles Times* that he prepared for the role by withdrawing in reclusion and focusing on study and meditation.

"I can say in truth that the playing of this part has affected my whole life and the impressions will never leave me," he stated. "I have tried earnestly and sincerely, with a deep prayer in my heart, to bring a message to the world, one which will reach, perhaps, millions. Now my only wish is that whoever may witness the performances of *Civilization* will realize only the truth and beauty of the message."

To be cruel, Fisher's wish did not come true. His Jesus lacked emotional authority and depth and he played the part like an automaton rather than as the force of love.

Also, having Jesus inhabit the count's body invests too much into the pacifist cause – oddly, the film is far more effective in its graphic presentation of the battlefield terrors, particularly scenes where soldiers pillage rural villages and prey on their residents, and the scenes with Ferdinand's melodramatic sermonizing are clumsy and heavy-handed.

Civilization was initially well received when it was released in 1916 – after all, that was the year when President Woodrow Wilson was running for re-election with assurances that he would not bring the isolationist practices of the country into World War I. But once Wilson changed his policy and put the United States into war in 1917, *Civilization* was quickly withdrawn from circulation. Over the years, the film's reputation suffered, especially when compared to Griffith's *Intolerance*. And while *Civilization* is, admittedly, artistically inferior to *Intolerance*, its bold use of Jesus as a character in a contemporary drama needs to be recognized and appreciated for being far ahead of its time.

Jesus Films in the 1920s

Jesus was absent from the screen during the last few years of the 1910s and returned to film in a segment of *Leaves from Satan's Book*, a 1920 Danish feature directed by Carl Theodor Dreyer. Very loosely adapted from the 1895 novel *The Sorrows of Satan* by British author Marie Corelli, the film envisions Satan exiled by God on Earth with the mission of overseeing temptations of historic figures during crucial points in time. Satan is given a somewhat strange sentence as part of his punishment: for every soul who embraces his evil temptation, 100 years are added to his earthbound exile. But for every soul who resists temptation, 1,000 years are erased from his sentence.

The film is divided into four segments, beginning with Jesus' arrival into Jerusalem and the angst felt by Judas over the direction of Jesus' ministry. Satan poses as a Pharisee – even going so far as to kiss the mezuzah at the entrance of the temple – and quickly picks up on Judas' presence and unhappiness. But this Satan is not pleased that his evil is being absorbed by Judas, for it means that his exile will be extended by a century. But Satan does not try to dissuade Judas from his actions, and even hands him the 30 pieces of silver while silently grieving for what had occurred.

This was Dreyer's third film as a director, and it probably would have been forgotten by cinema historians had it not been for the innovations offered in his later works. Neither this segment nor the others that follow – with Satan turning up in the Spanish Inquisition, the French Revolution and the 1917 Bolshevik uprising – are particularly memorable. Aside from taking an idiosyncratic position of making Satan a vaguely sympathetic entity, the portrayal of Jesus' betrayal is presented in a stiff, pageant-like manner that harkens back to the earliest days of the silent cinema rather than the more innovative nature of 1920s cinema.

Over in Germany, the first Jesus-centric film to be released was the 1921 production *Der Galiläer*, directed by the Russian-born Dimitri Buchowetzki, who worked in Berlin, Hollywood and London over the course of his career. *Der Galiläer* turned up in American theaters in 1928 under the title *The Passion Play*, but it failed to connect with audiences.

Today, *Der Galiläer* has a negative reputation among scholars of Jesus-centric cinema. Film scholar Matt Page viewed this production as being the one entry in Jesus-centric filmmaking of the silent years "that most unmistakably reflects the anti-Semitism that was rife in interwar Germany," adding that the Sanhedrin chieftains are presented by Buchowetzki in an intentionally hideous manner that "seem to comply with every anti-Semitic stereotype in the book." Another film scholar, Reinhold Zwick, complained that "while the Romans are exculpated of guilt in connection with the death of Jesus, the faction associated with the High Priest is presented as a bunch of hateful and devious bandits. In both their actions and their attitude, Caiaphas and his colleagues reflect a whole range of anti-Semitic stereotypes and serve as the striking example of anti-Jewish attitude reflected in some Christian visual tradition."

Der Galiläer survives in a 47-minute print restored by Germany's Bundesarchiv-filmarchiv, but outside of a German DVD release the film remains unknown in most countries. In view of the problematic reputation from its anti-Semitic tone, this is the rare case where obscurity is a blessing.

Two years after *Der Galiläer*, Robert Wiene, who put Germany on the global cinematic map with his 1920 masterpiece *The Cabinet of Dr. Caligari*, put forth *I.N.R.I.*, which offers a strange approach to the subject. Adapted from the 1905 novel by Peter Rosegger, *I.N.R.I.* is often more profane than sacred due to an emotionally frigid Expressionist presentation that is at odds with the spiritual and intellectual complexity of its holy inspiration.

Initially, Wiene planned to frame the ancient story with a modern narrative device of an incarcerated anarchist facing the death penalty who is told the story of Jesus by a prison chaplain. However, this approach raised complaints from German censors and it was dropped prior to the film's premiere.

Instead, *I.N.R.I.* introduces the infant Jesus already lying in the manger and under the adoring gaze of both humans and angels – the latter observants line the roof of the manger and play musical instruments while a large paper Star of Bethlehem dangles beside them. Jesus is then shown as a youth in the synagogue, confounding the elders with his knowledge. Mary (played by Henny Porten, who was one of Germany's most prominent film stars of the era) finds Him and looks skyward in a mix of dread and love.

From there, we are in Jesus' adult years. Pontius Pilate (Werner Krauss, Wiene's Dr. Caligari) is weary and dreary, and reacts to news of Jesus' growing popularity with mild indifference. More disturbed by Jesus' actions are the leaders of the Sanhedrin, who gather beneath an oversized anachronistic Star of David – that symbol was not present in the Bible-era, and it is not really needed because the stereotypical excesses in the appearance of the Sanhedrin leaders would have given audiences a far-too-easy clue for guessing their religion.

When the adult Jesus finally shows up, he is moving in a stiff gait with his arms by his side and a blank stare accentuated by dark rings around his eyes. Gregori Chmara, who played the title role in Wiene's 1922 *Raskolnikow*, was certainly the eeriest Jesus to appear on screen at the time, and he often comes across like the Judean ancestor of Conrad Veidt's Cesare the somnambulist in *The Cabinet of Dr. Caligari*. When Jesus gathers the children, the scene is unsettling because Chmara's Jesus is a sterile entity that has no visible signs of connection with the youngsters being embraced.

Outside of His mother Mary, the only easily recognizable figures surrounding Jesus in this film are Mary Magdalene (Asta Nielsen, another major star of German silent cinema) and Judas (Alexander Granach). Mary Magdalene has little to do except wash Jesus' feet and comfort Mary as Jesus' final days come about, but Judas shown to be is increasingly irritated by Jesus' behavior and succumbs to a pair of Sanhedrin chieftains who have been stalking him. When Judas betrays Jesus at the Last Supper, he inexplicably raises his arms in joy, as if celebrating some sort of scored goal.

Wiene set *I.N.R.I.* within highly stylized interior sets that don't bear much resemblance to the popular concept of ancient Palestine. Indeed, the Garden of Gethsemane looks like an alien landscape with bizarre overgrown foliage. The cold avant-garde nature of the production design is mirrored by ensemble acting that is stiff and flat for too much of the footage, creating a monotonous presentation that numbs the viewer.

Ironically, it is only when Jesus has been condemned to death on the cross that the film comes to life. Chmara's nearly lifeless Jesus suddenly channels the depths of unspeakable pain as his body is tortured by the Roman centurions. Chmara's eyes, which barely registered any sign of emotion before, brilliantly mirror the suffering and anguish that the physically broken and crucified Jesus is seen enduring. It is such a startling feat of acting that one has to wonder why Wiene waited so long before giving the actor the chance to unleash his talents. The film ends with the death of Chmara's Jesus on the cross – the absence of the Resurrection is unusual for a Jesus-centric film of that era.

I.N.R.I. was well received in Europe when it was first released, but Americans would not get to see it until 1933 when it had a limited stateside release stateside as *Crown of Thorns* with a synchronized music score. Today, it is difficult to appreciate *I.N.R.I.* because an extant and restored version is not readily available for public viewing. The complete film was considered lost for years, but in 1999 a copy was found in the silent film library Cineteca del Friuli in Italy. Another print was located in Tokyo in 2006. For most people, the only way to see the film today is via an incomplete version with Czech subtitles and an annoying time stamp, which can be found on YouTube.

Back in Hollywood, Metro-Goldwyn-Mayer decided to approach the subject, albeit through a popular novel and not an adaptation of the Gospels. MGM's lavish 1925 production of Lew Wallace's epic novel *Ben-Hur: A Tale of the Christ* was radically different from other genre films of this era by not having the adult Jesus as a full-frontal character in the drama. Instead, the film offered an infant Jesus in an opening Nativity sequence, although the child's face is not shown. Director Fred Niblo depicted the adult Jesus only by an outstretched hand that provides water to the enslaved Judah Ben-Hur, teaches the Sermon on the Mount, and heals the leprosy that deformed Judah's mother and sister. The actors in these scenes look off-screen in amazement at the holy presence before them, leaving the audience to speculate at the wonder they are missing.

The reticence to show Jesus on-screen is curious, as there was never any audience outrage before at having an on-screen Jesus. And considering the film's subtitle of "A Tale of the Christ," it feels peculiar to have an eponymous figure reduced to a hand that briefly stretches out across the screen. Indeed, most of the focus of the film is on spectacle rather than spiritualism, with the celebrated chariot race as the eye-popping centerpiece that ensured the film's critical and commercial success.

Film historians Pantelis Michelakis and Maria Wyke, writing in *The Ancient World in Silent Cinema*, speculated that this was designed to create a dramatic link between the sacred and the earth-bound, claiming that "Jesus is invisible, but active in the world." This effect would be repeated into the sound era when Hollywood epics with a Jesus-centric focus would inevitably keep Him as a faceless, voiceless bit player represented by the back of His head, an outstretched hand or a barely visible figure shot from a great distance.

The last major Jesus-focused film of the silent cinema era was Cecil B. DeMille's 1927 release *The King of Kings*. The production offered heaping servings of DeMille's vices and virtues as a filmmaker: an astonishing sense of visual spectacle and the uncanny ability to make an epic move at a swift pace, coupled with a bizarre sense of dramatic puerility laced with the obsessive need to improve upon holy source material with old-fashioned vulgarity.

DeMille had scored a major commercial success in 1923 with *The Ten Commandments*, which offered a diptych that matched the visually commanding epic tale of the Exodus against a modern morality play loaded with sex and violence. As a follow-up, the director/producer toyed with a film based on the Old Testament story of Noah but opted to switch to the New Testament when he discovered Warner Bros. was planning its own film about the Biblical deluge. Jeanie Macpherson, DeMille's favorite screenwriter, was tasked with adapting the Gospels according to Cecil B. DeMille.

From the opening scenes, *The King of Kings* decides to jazz up the story with some Roaring Twenties sex appeal. If we are to embrace this retelling, we need to accept Mary Magdalene as a glamorous and wealthy courtesan who has the richest Roman and Judean men at her command. Mary's palatial home includes muscular male attendants, a pet leopard and a wardrobe closer in style and spirit to the then-contemporary burlesque revues than the fashions of the Roman Empire.

But Mary is upset: her lover Judas Iscariot is spending more time with a mysterious carpenter who has become famous for miracle healings. Outraged at being dumped, Mary summons her zebra-borne chariot (a gift to her from a Nubian king) and drives off to reclaim Judas.

Rarely has a Biblical film taken so many zany liberties as this opening sequence in *The King of Kings*, but DeMille somehow manages to pull it off – and in fairness, DeMille avoids conflating Mary Magdalene with the woman accused of adultery, who appears later in her own segment. The opening sequence was shot in the two-strip Technicolor process that gives Mary's domain a brilliantly tawdry setting, and the dramatic seething of Jacqueline Logan as the spurned harlot is quite entertaining for all the wrong reasons.

But *The King of Kings* does not turn Jesus' life into a boulevard farce, and the introduction of Jesus to the audience comes in a startling manner. A lame boy named Mark is healed by Jesus – the intertitles insist that the child grew up to write the Gospel According to Mark, another obvious anachronism. The boy brings a blind girl to Jesus' presence – we know she is blind because she walks around with shut eyes and outstretched hands, complaining that she cannot see. But when her eyes finally open, the camera takes on her point of view to present Jesus for the first time.

DeMille cast English actor H.B. Warner as Jesus – at 50, Warner was somewhat too old for the role, but through expert make-up and DeMille's direction, he brought a sense of mature wisdom to the character. The intellectual serenity in Warner's interpretation is in striking contrast to the rest of the cast, who either seem to be on the verge of a nervous breakdown or are emoting with enough fury to fuel 10 silent films.

Mary Magdalene's initial hostile confrontation with Jesus sets the stage for one of the most striking sequences ever captured in a DeMille film. Recognizing the cause of her sins, Jesus calmly but firmly evicts seven demons from her body. This was achieved in a brilliant special effects sequence involving multiple exposures, with the demons depicted as wretched women embodying each of the Seven Deadly Sins – another anachronism, admittedly, but one that fits in the context of the story. Warner's Jesus is the calm amidst Logan's emotional storm, and her transformation after the exorcism is a great feat of acting. Sadly, Mary Magdalene's character mostly vanishes from this point in the story and only returns in the final scenes of the film.

There is another unexpected surprise sequence where DeMille gives Jesus a sense of playful nostalgia. While entering a carpenter's shop, Jesus smiles in recollection of his pre-ministerial career and picks up the tools that were once part of his trade. He begins to smooth out the rough edges of a long wooden plank – the end of the plank is behind a curtain that Jesus initially does not notice. When the curtain is pulled back, Jesus discovers that He was smoothing down a giant cross that the carpenter had been contracted to make by the Romans. But rather than go for the obvious and have Jesus do a double-take or worse, DeMille allows Warner's Jesus to calmly stare at the cross, showing no outward signs of acquaintance to His fate.

The cross later returns in the sequence where Jesus is marched by His Roman captors to Calvary. Again, DeMille's odd dichotomy of sublime and ridiculous is on display: the boy Mark watches Jesus drag the cross and begins to berate the powerfully-built Simon of Cyrene (played by William Boyd, the future Hopalong Cassidy) to volunteer to carry the cross for the scourged and exhausted Jesus. Simon steps forward when Jesus is unable to proceed with His labor and goes to lift the cross. But the cross is significantly heavier than Simon expected and he is not initially able to shoulder the burden. In surprise, he turns and views the thin and badly tortured Jesus, clearly baffled how someone who appears physically weak was able to drag the heavy cross for such a long period. With profound new respect for Jesus, Simon manages to raise the cross and complete Jesus' trek to Calvary.

Nonetheless, DeMille's bad instincts often get in the way. Prior to the Crucifixion, DeMille and his scenarist Macpherson turn Pilate's judgment of Christ into a near-soap opera. Jesus' time before Herod Antipas is omitted, while Pilate's rather sexy wife (identified in the intertitles as Claudia Procula, a name that is not in the New Testament) makes a full-throttle direct appeal for Jesus in front of all gathered, rather than sending a messenger with a note asking that He be spared. The high priest Caiaphas hovers around Pilate, sneering and manipulating him to pass fatal judgment against Jesus. And when the decree for Crucifixion is announced, Judas Iscariot comes running into the room and returns his pieces of silver to Caiaphas, grabbing the rope that was used to bind Jesus' wrists and turning it into a noose for his own destruction.

DeMille and Macpherson opted to make Caiaphas the central villain of *The King of Kings*, and this is the biggest problem with the film. The make-up and costuming for Rudolph Schildkraut's interpretation of the villainous high priest pushed the proverbial envelope on Jewish stereotyping. The film also creates a new scene where Caiaphas reacts to an earthquake that followed the Crucifixion by pleading to God that he alone was responsible for Jesus' death and that the guilt of the murder should not fall on the Jewish people. This aspect of *The King of Kings* brought more than a few critical comments from Jewish-American leaders, although DeMille vehemently insisted that his film was not anti-Semitic.

"Jewish editors and Rabbis in some instances have read Anti-Semitic ideas into their interpretation of my picture because they are not acquainted with what the New Testament tells us," DeMille said in a statement following negative criticism from Jewish leaders. "They have out of their own minds invented a hostility that does not exist. The danger now is that some Christian editor or other will say that the Jews' reaction to *The King of Kings* springs from a guilty conscience and consequently they will infer that if Jesus were alive today these Jews, I speak of would crucify him again. The very men who read prejudice into the picture are themselves storing up material for anti-Semitic propaganda. They are the ones who will be entirely responsible for any prejudice against the Jewish people. *The King of Kings* does not in any manner encourage such prejudice. It tells the immortal story without any racial implications whatsoever and shows the Jews divided into opposing parties over the reforms urged by Jesus."

However, DeMille agreed to edit the film to tone down the perceived stereotyping of Sanhedrin leadership when the film was being prepared for European distribution.

If DeMille was guilty of anything, it was being something of a cornball. In the Calvary sequence, he not only placed Jesus' mother Mary at the foot of His cross, but also placed the grieving elderly mother of one of the crucified thieves, along with the agitated pet dog of the other thief, at the feet of their respective crosses. There is also an unsympathetic woman watching the three men die while eating popcorn – don't ask how she managed to bring that Mexican snack to ancient Judea.

For the Resurrection, DeMille brought back the two-strip Technicolor from the opening sequence. But whereas DeMille used overheated color to emphasis the luxuriant sinfulness of the pre-cured Mary Magdalene, he also used the warmth and richness of the color cinematography to emphasis the power and serenity of the resurrected Jesus. The style employed in the ending of *The King of Kings* almost justifies the sometimes-baffling means that led up to the moving denouement.

The original 1927 road show presentation of *The King of Kings* ran for 155 minutes, but a 1928 general release version cut 40 minutes of footage and switched out the Technicolor version of the opening sequence for a black-and-white tableau. The shorter version was the one that was rereleased with a synchronized music score and sound effects in the 1930s and was broadcast for years on television. Fortunately, the 155-minute version was preserved and shown again in 2004 for a DVD release from The Criterion Collection.

The King of Kings was not the last feature-length Jesus-focused film of the silent era. That distinction went to *Jesus of Nazareth*, a six-reel, independently-made low-budget feature starring Dutch actor Philip Van Loan in the title role. Details on *Jesus of Nazareth* are scant – film scholar Terris C. Howard has credited the direction to Anders Van Haven, an actor who directed silent films under the pseudonym William A. Howell, and there is documentation to affirm that some of the film was shot near New Orleans.

Unfortunately, this small production was overshadowed by the DeMille extravaganza and had only a scant release before disappearing from theaters. It eventually disappeared forever, as no extant print is currently available for review; copies of the film bearing its title are in the possession of the Library of Congress and the UCLA Film and Television Archive, but that footage belongs to a re-release of the 1912 *From the Manger to the Cross*.

Robert Henderson-Bland as Jesus in From the Manger to the Cross *(1912).*

Chapter Two: Jesus Arrives in Sound Films

"And suddenly there came from heaven a noise like a violent rushing wind, and it filled the whole house where they were sitting."
– Acts 2:2

Filmmakers had been experimenting with the incorporation of sound into cinematic exhibition from the beginning of the art form, but it would take years before a viable solution could be made available for commercial distribution. The box office success of *The Jazz Singer*, the 1927 feature starring Al Jolson that peppered songs and a brief slice of dialogue into a mostly silent film, signaled the dawning of a new era in filmmaking – the "talkies" would become the new normal and the big screen would no longer be absent of the human voice.

But this created a problem for any filmmaker who wanted to adapt the life of Jesus. For starters, what would Jesus sound like? And would audiences laugh or be offended if the actor portraying Jesus spoke in an accent or a manner that seemed out of context with the solemnity of the subject?

For the early part of the 1930s, film distributors felt it was safer to dust off silent Jesus-centric films and re-release them with new synchronized music scores. And while these films managed to squeeze out a few extra dollars at the box office, it became obvious that the holy subject would eventually have to be put in front of both a camera and a microphone.

The first feature-length production of the sound film era to incorporate Jesus Christ into the on-screen characters came about in 1933, but it was not inspired by the Gospels. Instead, it was based on a weird legend that originated in the 13th century and percolated across Europe well into the early 20th century.

The story of The Wandering Jew involved a Jewish witness to the Crucifixion who denigrated Jesus while He carried the cross to Calvary. In this tale, Jesus responded to the insult in a decidedly non-Christ-like manner: He put a curse on the smart-aleck that

Robert Le Vigan in Julien Duvivier's 1935 Golgotha.

locked him in immortality until the day of the Second Coming. Thus, the Jewish man would never be able to grow old and die and was thus forced to move endlessly from land to land before people got wise to the true nature of his identity.

The Wandering Jew legend turned up over the centuries in works by such notable writers as Percy Bysshe Shelley, Nathaniel Hawthorne, Mark Twain, O. Henry and Guillaume Apollinaire. Georges Méliès created a short film in 1904 based on the story, and British playwright E. Temple Thurston created a script that was the basis of a 1923 silent film. In 1933, Britain's Twickenham Film Studios decided to brush off the Thurston drama for a sound film remake.

However, there were new issues in 1933 that did not exist during the silent era. British censors prevented any locally-produced film from having an on-screen actor provide a face or voice to the character of Jesus. Considering that Jesus was crucial to this particular story that might seem more than a little problematic for viewers. Furthermore, the ascension of Adolf Hitler as Germany's chancellor cast a shadow on any film about European Jewry – especially one with a negative depiction of the Jewish population.

To its credit, Twickenham scored a casting coup by bringing in the great German actor Conrad Veidt to play the title character in his version of *The Wandering Jew*. Veidt gained international recognition in 1920 as the homicidal somnambulist in *The Cabinet of Dr. Caligari*, and he was among the first creative artists to emigrate from Germany when the Nazi Party took control. (Veidt's wife Ilona Prager was Jewish and he refused to divorce her in order to remain active in his nation's entertainment industry.) Veidt's resettlement in Britain would be used to push back at any potential charges of an anti-Semitic tone being present in *The Wandering Jew*, while the actor's pronounced German accent also separated his Jewish character in the film from the Gentile characters who spoke with posh British theatrical accents.

The Wandering Jew opens in Jerusalem on the day of Jesus' death. Veidt plays Matathias, a wealthy Jewish aristocrat whose lover Judith is dying in his house from some undefined illness. Judith begs Matathias to fetch Jesus to cure her, but he is resistant. "The son of a carpenter – what does he know about healing?" Matathias sneers.

Matathias goes out and witnesses an off-screen Jesus carrying the cross to Golgotha. He calls to Jesus to heal Judith, and a light suddenly shines on him from Jesus' direction while an intertitle flashes on screen that reads, "Return the woman to her husband and she will be cured." (The intertitle was the filmmakers' way of circumventing the British censors' ban on a walking-talking Jesus.) The crowd watching Jesus' fate laughs at Matathias, who heads home. He later returns to watch Jesus' journey to Golgotha. Matathias spits in the direction of Jesus, and the off-screen light flashes on Matathias again while another intertitle flashes on screen that reads, "I will not wait for you but you shall wait for me until I come for you again." Matathias returns to his home and finds Judith has died. Grief-stricken, he takes out his dagger to kill himself, but his act of self-immolation is stopped when the dagger breaks in half upon impacting his flesh. Matathias realizes the meaning of Jesus' curse.

The film then flashes forward some 1,300 years, when a mysterious knight is following the Crusaders in their effort to conquer the Holy Land. An elderly Jewish man approaches the Crusaders' camp – he is referred to simply as "Jew" by the knights – and identifies the stranger in armor as the Wandering Jew of legend. Matathias is now clean-shaven but looks the same as he did on the day of the Crucifixion. He is also a lascivious wolf on the prowl for married women. When the wife of a Crusader falls under his spell, Matathias tells his servant, "Should the husband follow, I would not like even his death to disturb me."

However, this rendezvous goes badly – the woman recoils after making lip contact and cries out, "To think that mine have touched those lips that spat on Christ!" She then discovers her husband is dead outside of Matathias' tent. His cover blown, Matathias makes an exit and turns up two centuries later as a Sicilian merchant.

Life in Sicily is not copacetic for Matathias: his wife has become an obsessed Catholic who wants to enter a convent when their young son dies from an adder's bite. When he tries to convince his wife not to become a nun, she responds: "If you were to kill me now, I should still be with Him." Accepting the burden of his curse, Matathias moves on and turns up in late 15th century Spain during the Inquisition as a doctor. He treats a prostitute for an ankle injury,

but through a strange turn of events he winds up before the inquisi-
tors' court and admits to being a Jew. The Inquisition's executioners
tie him to a stake in a crucifixion position and Matathias finally
atones for his bad behavior toward Jesus, proclaiming, "Thou hast
come to me...again." Jesus appears as a flash of overhead light and
releases Matathias from the curse. Matathias dies peacefully at the
stake before suffering the pain of the Inquisition's fire.

The Wandering Jew is typical of a lot of early 1930s British films:
a creaky production marred by stagnant visuals and a broad style
of acting that might have worked on stage but seems overdone
when magnified by the camera. Veidt's proficiency in English was
not perfected and much of his line delivery comes across wavering
between uncertain and sterile. Future British screen icons such as
Frances L. Sullivan and Felix Aylmer were among Matathias' persecutors in the Spanish segment, while a very young and sexy Peggy
Ashcroft played the prostitute that sped up the title character's ultimate demise – but none of these great talents could spin gold from
the leaden dialogue that they were handed.

From a contemporary standpoint, it is difficult to appreciate the
resolution of *The Wandering Jew*, with Matathias belatedly embrac-
ing the spirit of Jesus, especially since the forced conversion of Jews
into Christianity has been a sore point of interfaith relations for
years. From a Christian standpoint, the notion that Jesus would
aggressively and sadistically punish His adversaries is antithetical
to the core concept of the Gospels.

British audiences in 1933 viewed a 110-minute version of the
film. Metro-Goldwyn-Mayer sought the American distribution for
the film, but the Hollywood censors at the Motion Picture Producers and Distributors of America – those humorless souls behind
the Production Code – were aghast at the film's contents and would
not allow the full version to be shown. Jewish advocacy groups got
wind of the film and vocally protested against its exhibition, and
the studio decided to drop plans for a theatrical release. A truncated
78-minute version was approved by the censors for U.S. release, but
no major studio would touch it. A tiny art house distributor named
Olympic Pictures acquired the production and gave it the briefest
and scantest of releases.

The first film of the sound era to give audiences a walking-talking Jesus was the French film from 1935 called *Golgotha*, directed by Julien Duvivier, who is best remembered today for the 1937 classic *Pépé le Moko*, the 1942 all-star Hollywood film *Tales of Manhattan,* and the 1948 British version of *Anna Karenina* starring Vivien Leigh. Looking back, it made sense for the French to make the first sound film about Jesus – as cited earlier, many of the first silent narrative films on the subject were created in France in the late 1890s.

This production was fairly elaborate by the standards of mid-1930s French cinema, with an extravagant budget that enabled location shooting in Algiers (substituting for Old Jerusalem), massive sets and multitudes of extras. Duvivier might have assumed that the film would have a strong attractiveness in the global movie market, which explains why there are lengthy pauses in between dialogue exchanges and many scenes where there is much commotion but no talk.

Viewed today, *Golgotha* is strange because Jesus is barely present in the first part of the film. More than a quarter-hour passes before He is glimpsed, albeit from a distance amid the multitudes that welcome His entry into Jerusalem. Jesus' face and voice are kept from the viewer until roughly the half-hour mark with the clearing of the Temple, at which point he is revealed as a somber, strangely mysterious figure. Robert Le Vigan, who was a minor actor in French films before being cast, is a startling vision as Jesus, with pale skin and haunted eyes – from appearances, this Jesus appears to be living with daily emotional torture. His prayer in Gethsemane is so drenched in sorrow that the moment is among the most heartbreaking scenes ever filmed.

Sadly, too much of the film is polluted by unapologetically broad caricatures of the Sanhedrin leaders and their villainous plotting against Jesus. Lumbering about the proceedings is Lucas Gridoux as a too-obvious Judas – his angst is heavily externalized in comparison to Le Vigan's subtle internalized suffering – and Jean Gabin (with a silly haircut) as an indolent Pilate. The film gives a surprisingly decent amount of time to Pilate's wife (played with a healthy dose of passion by Edwige Feuillère), and the delivery and dismissal of her written message to Pilate during the trial of Jesus is prominently included in the film.

Golgotha manages to right itself when Jesus is arrested and judged. Harry Baur's Herod Antipas is a foolish, silly figure whose mocking of Jesus seems more playful than malicious. The scourging is mostly conducted off-screen, with a crowd of sadistic onlookers watching with glee through the prison bars at the torture. And perhaps the most striking scene is when Jesus fails to recognize His mother on the road to Cavalry – tortured into exhaustion, He stares out at his collapsing world with hollowed eyes and a shell-shocked composure.

Duvivier offers two striking effects in the post-Crucifixion moments: a feminine angelic voice calmly informs the startled women at the tomb that Jesus has risen, and the final shot with two of the Calvary crosses taken down and carried away by Roman soldiers while the third cross – obviously, the structure used to kill Jesus – remaining in a ghostly silhouette against the sky.

In its time, *Golgotha* was hailed as a major accomplishment. An English-dubbed version was released in the U.S. in 1937 and was praised by the National Board of Review as being among the year's best foreign films. In the late 1940s, an edited version of the English-dubbed presentation was broadcast by several U.S. television stations.

But, over time, *Golgotha* developed serious reputational problems. Chief among these was the off-screen life of Le Vigan, who openly supported the Nazi occupation of France during World War II and was arrested and jailed after the war for his collaboration with the Germans. Many postwar film scholars also condemned *Golgotha* for seeming to place the responsibility of Jesus' death primarily on the Jews of ancient Jerusalem.

Ben McCann, a Duvivier biographer, wisely pinpointed where *Golgotha* ultimately missed the mark. "He does not focus on what Jesus says or does," McCann wrote about Duvivier. "Rather, he depicts how others (Judas, Pilate, Herod, Caiaphas, the Disciples at Emmaus) see Him. That reflection is manifested in the title, which expands the narrative from a person to a place while also calling attention to the narrative's pre-ordained endpoint."

Elsewhere in 1935 was the first Hollywood sound film with Jesus as a character – sort of. The RKO Radio Pictures epic *The Last Days of Pompeii* was helmed by Merian C. Cooper and Ernest B. Schoedsack, the creators of *King Kong*, and they borrowed the title of Edward Bulwer-Lytton's celebrated book without bothering to take the contents.

In this film, a Pompeiian blacksmith named Marcus (Preston Foster) becomes a gladiator after his wife and infant son are killed in a chariot accident. After a career-ending injury, the gladiator becomes a slave trader and is later employed by Pontius Pilate (Basil Rathbone) as a horse thief. While in Judea, the young adopted son of this blacksmith-gladiator-slave trader-horse thief is severely wounded in a riding accident. The locals recommend bringing the child to "the master" for healing.

Jesus is not identified by name in this film, nor do we see or hear Him. Instead, the healing occurs when a bright light shines from off-screen on the dumbfounded Marcus and the injured child, who instantly regains his health. Later in the film, Marcus watches the procession to Cavalry from a distance, refusing to come to the aid of the condemned man. As Marcus leaves Jerusalem, three crosses can be seen on Calvary, which is made to look like a soaring mountain.

The Last Days of Pompeii fast-forwards to the healed youth aiding Christian slaves who escaped the arena run by Marcus. The eruption of Mount Vesuvius puts an end to Pompeii, with Marcus displaying some severely belated altruism by sacrificing himself in order to enable the Christian slaves to sail off to safety. As Marcus lays dying, a transparent image of Jesus appears to him – and then the story abruptly ends.

Cooper and Schoedsack moved the Vesuvius eruption back several decades to accommodate the trial and execution of Jesus into their story's time frame. And while Basil Rathbone made Pilate into a surprisingly complex character – an intellectual cad in his horse theft antics, an emotionally anguished judge aware that he has sentenced an innocent to death – the rest of the film is marred by hammy acting and a surprisingly underwhelming special effects finale.

American filmmakers stayed away from the subject until 1939, when an Episcopal priest from Red Wing, Minnesota, named James K. Friedrich brought forth *The Great Commandment*, a $130,000 feature-length production, as the first offering of his start-up company Cathedral Films. The film created a bidding war among the major Hollywood studios, with 20th Century- Fox paying $200,000 for the rights to this production. However, the studio was not interested in releasing Friedrich's production, but instead in shooting a big-budget remake that would star Tyrone Power, its top box office attraction.

After two years, 20th Century-Fox had yet to start work on the Tyrone Power version. With nothing to show for its investment, the studio dumped *The Great Commandment* with relatively little fanfare in theaters.

Despite its shaky back story, *The Great Commandment* is important from a historical perspective because it was the first American film of the sound era where Jesus Christ plays a significant role in the story. Unfortunately, Jesus wound up being shoehorned into a film that pinballed between mediocrity and unintentional humor.

The film is set in 30 A.D. in an unnamed Judean town "between Jericho and Jerusalem" (according to the opening intertitles). The Roman occupation force is not creating much pleasure for the local population, who balk at the empire's excessive taxation and brutal military power structure. The arrival in the town of a centurion leader named Longinus brings about new resentment against the Romans. A band of rebels who call themselves zealots are plotting an uprising, and this particular town is home to a pair of zealot leaders: Joel and his younger brother Zadok, who are the sons of the rabbi Lamech. This family is a bit on the strange side: Lamech speaks with a heavy Eastern European accent and wears an extraordinarily bushy beard while his sons are curiously clean-shaven and give off the impression of being All-American *goyishe* guys. This is no surprise when one considers Yiddish theater star Maurice Moscovich plays the rabbi and the decidedly non-Yiddish John Beal and Warren McCullum are cast as his offspring.

For the first hour of the film, Joel and Zadok bicker about when to lead a rebellion against the Romans, pausing only to allow Joel to moon over the fair Tamar, who is in love with him. But the rabbi wants to send Joel to Jerusalem for his studies, so he arranges with Tamar's father for Zadok to marry the young woman instead. With his heart broken by this turn of events, Joel then launches a new scheme: to reject his father's plans for an education and go out to recruit a new leader for the zealots. His choice is a carpenter from Nazareth who is reportedly getting a lot of attention from the Judean people.

Up until this point, *The Great Commandment* has little going for it. The acting is weak, bordering on amateurish, the script is silly, the direction by Irving Pichel is enervated and the production – which was shot at the Selznick International studios during the same time that *Gone with the Wind* was being made – looks cheap. And then, with the arrival of Jesus, a celluloid miracle happens and the film suddenly becomes a little more interesting.

Jesus is first seen very briefly as a reflection in a pond – it is startling to see the face of Jesus on the American screen again, although the actor in the shot is not identified in the credits. From there, the camera takes a POV shot from Jesus' perspective as He offers wise insight to the Disciples and travelers gathered around. (Director Pichel, who was a character actor before becoming an expert behind the camera, took on the voice performance of Jesus and offered eloquent line readings.) Joel presents Jesus with his sword, but Jesus responds with the Matthew 26:52 message regarding what becomes of those who live by the sword. Joel is perplexed and initially disappointed when the disciple Andrew explains Jesus' nonviolence. But the disciple Judas then tells Joel that he can get Jesus to see the value of the zealot movement.

Joel returns to his town to witness the marriage of Tamar and Zadok. The rabbi is glad that Joel has returned but is appalled that he has been influenced by Jesus. Jesus abruptly arrives in the town and the rabbi tries to quiz him on religious piety. Jesus (presented again in a POV shot and in a brief glimpse as a shadow on a wall) offers the parable of the Good Samaritan, which leaves the rabbi and other doubters of Jesus' wisdom confused and agitated.

From here, the story really goes off the rails. Zadok decides to forego his wedding night celebration to murder the centurion Longinus. In the scuffle that ensues, Zadok is killed and Longinus is knocked unconscious and is badly injured. Joel, who is moved by the Good Samaritan parable, tends to the suffering Longinus, to the horror of his father and the townspeople. The centurion forces arrive just as Longinus awakes to discover Joel has been caring for him. Longinus orders the centurions to arrest and imprison Joel.

The film then switches to a Jerusalem prison cell where Joel is berated by a guard who complains about missing a crucifixion that took place earlier. Longinus shows up in Joel's cell carrying a spear – the centurion explains that he had Joel imprisoned to save him from the fury of his townspeople, although he never explains why Joel was kept stuck behind bars for so long after the incident had passed. Longinus asks why Joel would treat a perceived enemy with such kindness, and Joel cites Jesus' teaching. Can you guess whose crucifixion took place that day and which centurion stuck his spear into the side of the dying man on the cross? If that's not enough, Tamar shows up, clearly not mourning Zadok's death. Joel, Tamar and Longinus decide to go back to Joel's town and preach the message that Jesus sought to spread.

It might be too flippant to walk away from *The Great Commandment* muttering "Father, forgive them, for they do not know what they are doing." In fairness, the film had the courage to break an unofficial taboo relating to Biblical films. With the introduction of the 1934 Production Code, Hollywood films had to adhere to very strict guidelines on the presentation of religious material. But there was no specific guideline in the code on how Jesus could be presented on the screen. Friedrich negotiated with the Breen Office (the purveyor of the Production Code) on the compromise presented here.

At the same time *The Great Commandment* was being readied for theatrical release, Cathedral Films also produced a series of Jesus-inspired short films designed for 16mm distribution to church groups and 8mm distribution to the home movie market. These films were made on budgets between $9,000 and $12,000 and were released without cast or crew credits, although it is known that Friedrich's daughter Martha was recruited as the infant Jesus for *The Child of Bethlehem*, marking the first time that the Son of God was played on-screen by a female. The company's 1942 *No*

Greater Power offered Nelson Leigh as the first adult actor to portray Jesus as a facially visible and talking presence in an American film. Because these films were not intended to be shown in theater, they did not need to meet Production Code standards.

The Great Commandment was not the only film about Jesus made in 1939. *The Life and Passion of the Christ* was produced in Egypt, making it the first film about Jesus produced in the Middle East. Details on this film are mostly elusive, although it is known that Mohamed Abdel Gawa was the film's director and Qadeer Ahmed Allam played Jesus. The film was created for Egypt's Coptic Christian minority for screenings at Christmas and Easter. Film historian Peter T. Chattaway stated the Egyptian government banned screenings in the 1970s – and since the film was never shown outside of Egypt, it is difficult to determine the artistic value of this endeavor or to confirm if prints still survive.

The 1940s and Jesus on Screen

Another film to incorporate Jesus into its story broke a significant barrier in having the holy figure within the parameters of an all-Black cast. Barely acknowledged by the film world in its time but now considered a landmark in independent production, *The Blood of Jesus* fell from 1941 into a genre known as "race films" which featured all-Black casts and were shown exclusively in cinemas within predominantly black communities. Most of these films were directed by white filmmakers, but *The Blood of Jesus* was different because it was directed and scripted by Spencer Williams, a Black actor who worked his way up through the ranks of the race film world to become one of the very few African Americans to direct feature films in the 1940s.

Filmed in Texas on a $5,000 budget, *The Blood of Jesus* takes places in an unnamed Southern rural village with an all-Black population. A local church group is going to the river for baptismal services, and one of the people getting a religious immersion is the lovely newlywed Martha (Cathryn Caviness, in her only film performance). Absent from the service is her husband Razz (played Williams), who spent the day hunting (or poaching, it appears).

Martha is a devout Christian who wears a cross around her neck and admires a framed picture of Jesus hanging in her bedroom. Razz, however, is not one for religion and is not shy about showing contempt to his wife's faith.

The film's central drama occurs when Razz's gun accidentally discharges and Martha is shot. Her church group gathers around her bedside, singing hymns while Razz finds himself in a rare prayer session with the big man upstairs. A female angel comes to visit Martha and takes her soul from the bed on a journey to the crossroads between Hell and Zion. The angel warns Martha that the Devil will be after her, and almost immediately Satan appears (played by a cackling James B. Jones wearing a Halloween devil costume). The Devil sends his handsome lieutenant Judas Green to woo Martha to join him at a nightclub in the evil city. She agrees, only to find Judas has sold her to the owner of a seedy juke joint, where she is expected to engage in criminal practices with the male customers.

Martha escapes and returns to the crossroads, pursued by men from the juke joint who mistake her for a pickpocket. At the crossroads, however, a directional sign pointing out the paths to Hell and Zion turns into a giant crucifix, complete with a statue of Christ at its apex. The Devil approaches Martha, but the voice of Christ intervenes. (Jesus is dubbed by Williams on the soundtrack, his native Louisiana accent very pronounced.) Jesus intones, "Get thee behind me, Satan, for thou art now on holy ground."

The Devil exits, but a gang of men from the juke joint arrive on the scene, ready to stone Martha. This quickly turns into a riff on the woman accused of adultery, with the men speaking directly to the off-screen Jesus before being warned away about casting stones unless they were absent of sin.

With all of Martha's tormentors banished from her sight, a white-robed choir appears to sing "Steal Away to Jesus." Martha looks up to the figure of Jesus on the cross and mouths her gratitude to Jesus' protection. Martha lays her head on the stones at the foot of the cross and the blood of Christ slowly drips down from the crucified figure and runs thin rivulets across her face.

Martha wakes up in her bed and is reunited with her newly pious husband, who fervently offered his own prayers for her recovery. As

Martha and Razz embrace as a newly united couple with a shared faith, an angel appears to bless their future while the framed picture of Jesus hangs behind them on the wall.

Running a mere 58 minutes, *The Blood of Jesus* is a seriously imperfect film. Some footage was obviously misappropriated from other films and shoehorned into the flick, most notably a dream sequence from the 1911 silent *L'Inferno* that shows souls ascending to Heaven – the luxurious artistic imagery of that segment looks wildly out of place with the unpolished visual style in Williams' cheaply-made endeavor. Also, the costumed performers dressed as an angel and as the Devil makes for a simplistic Passion Play, and Williams' ridiculously small budget forced him to work with mostly amateur performers whose acting skills were not always at top grade.

But even if the production was burdened by poverty, the genuine and sincere display of Christian faith throughout the film is extremely rare for its time – and the scene with Jesus' blood dropping on Martha's face is truly startling. The film also displays a rich soundtrack filled with traditional gospel songs and an unapologetic affirmation of the power of Christ. No other film of its time, either within the restricted "race films" genre or even the more influential Hollywood output, came close to displaying its Christian faith in such a clear manner.

Williams would follow up *The Blood of Jesus* with two more faith-based films – the 1942 *Brother Martin: Servant of Jesus*, a biographical drama on Martin de Porres, a biracial Peruvian saint (this film, sadly, is considered lost) and the 1944 *Go Down, Death!* with Williams casting himself as a disreputable pastor. Williams directed several additional films ranging from farce to melodrama until 1947 but was not known to the wider public until he was cast in 1951 as Andy in the CBS television version of *Amos 'n' Andy*.

Although *The Blood of Jesus* was a popular title with the segregated Black audiences of the 1940s, it was unknown to white audiences and filmmakers, and its historic value in the evolution of Christ-focused cinema was not recognized until many years after its release, when film scholars tracing the African American presence in the film industry offered praise on Williams' ability to work with a miniscule budget and no formal filmmaking training. *Village Voice* critic J. Hoberman equated the film's raw power with folk art, while *Time*'s Richard Corliss praised it for possessing "naive grandeur." In 1991, the film was included on the Library of Congress' National Film Registry of "culturally, historically, or aesthetically significant films."

In 1942, the Mexican film industry took its first focus on Jesus' life with *Jésus de Nazareth*. Within its country of origin, the film's importance warranted enthusiasm from no less a figure than Luis M. Martinez, the Archbishop of Mexico City, who appears in the pre-credit sequence to explain the value of the production.

By contemporary standards, *Jésus de Nazareth* is a difficult film to watch. This was clearly a work of great sincerity, but good intentions do not always translate into quality filmmaking. With the exception of a few striking moments, the film feels like a recording of a community theater production, complete with cheapjack production settings and a cast that is not up to the holy source material.

Jésus de Nazareth omits Jesus' birth and childhood, introducing Him as an adult encountering John the Baptist. His initial presence on-screen is framed artistically via a reflection in the River Jordan, and Jesus' baptism is shot in a tight close-up with light shining from behind His head. But the sequence is much too polite – John the Baptist is uncommonly mild-mannered, despite his white fur toga and long hair, while Jesus moves with a stiff formality that almost seems mechanical. It also doesn't help that the baptism is staged on a patently phony set and that the men are wearing shabby wigs and none-too-convincing paste-on beards.

Almost immediately, Jesus has gathered his 12 Disciples and delivers the Sermon on the Mount. He heals a crippled man and then engages in a surprisingly lengthy encounter with the Woman at the Well. Jesus then encounters a blind man and another crippled man, but before He can heal them there is a chaotic noise happening off-screen – it's the woman accused of adultery, followed by the crowd of would-be stone throwers. After Jesus makes that classic comment about those without sin, the crowd scatters and the once-naughty woman surveys a street full of stones with no one to throw them.

Mercifully, the film does not conflate the accused adulteress with Mary Magdalene, but the latter turns up as a woman of great wealth who luxuriates in material splendor while surrounded by attractive young ladies who wait on her. This appears to be a riff on Cecil B. DeMille's vision of Mary of Magdalene as a wealthy courtesan in the 1927 *King of Kings* – except in the Mexican film, there is not a blatant identification of that profession. Mary Magdalene spies Jesus walking by her residence and goes outside to greet Him – and after a couple of minutes of conversation, she foregoes her bad-girl life to follow the Nazarene.

Of course, we can't forget Lazarus, and Jesus arrives to bring him back from the dead. This sequence is unintentionally funny when Jesus, Mary Magdalene and the Disciples follow Lazarus' sisters Mary and Martha into the small cave that houses the tomb – the surplus number of people creates a claustrophobic setting, and the raising of the dead man is depicted by a bright light shining underneath the lid of Lazarus' tomb. With that miracle, everyone in the cramped tomb drops to their knees in unison and genuflects to Jesus.

Needless to say, Jesus is not entirely welcome in Jerusalem, and He encounters a Sanhedrin wearing stereotypically exaggerated make-up and costuming that would appeal to a Neo-Nazi audience – Caiaphas even has a hat with goat-style horns. While the film spends a considerable amount of attention on the Passion, it curiously skips the Resurrection – instead, a glowing Jesus turns up alive almost immediately after dying on the cross while the soundtrack is flooded with Handel's "Hallelujah Chorus."

Jesus was played by José Cibrián, an Argentine actor. For much of the film, he walks with his right hand held on his chest, as if trying to calm an acid reflux flare-up. Cibrián mostly avoids displays of emotion, creating a robotic Jesus with a curiously blank look. It is not until the Passion that he shows any signs of dramatic power, and at that point he compensates for his earlier indifference – Cibrián suffers mightily, and the physical agony of his Jesus is so startling that it is hard to understand the indifference that came before these sequences. Unfortunately, no one else in the film bothers to offer anything that could be mistaken for a performance, creating an exercise in ecumenical ennui.

Jésus de Nazareth was directed by José Díaz Morales, a Spanish writer-director who went into Mexican exile after the Spanish Civil War. For *Jésus de Nazareth*, he tries to camouflage the poverty of this low-budget effort by jamming extras together and raising the decibel level on the soundtrack, thus trying to give the impression of much larger crowds. He continued directing into the 1970s and is best known outside of Mexico for helming several action romps featuring the popular masked wrestler Santo.

Jésus de Nazareth was never released in the U.S. with English subtitles and it is difficult to ascertain whether it played in U.S. theaters in the 1940s that catered to Spanish-speaking audiences – if it did, it escaped notice of the English-language media of that era. *Jésus de Nazareth* was a very popular film when it was released in Mexico, and its commercial success helped fuel a flurry of Mexican productions based on the New Testament, including *Queen of Queens: The Virgin Mary* (1945), *María Magdalena* (1945) ... *And He Died for Us* (1951) and *The Martyr of Calvary* (1952). Mexican cinema seemed to lose interest in the Holy Story until the 1966 *El Proceso de Cristo*. In the early 1970s, director Alejandro Galindo created a trilogy featuring *Jesus the Child God, Jesus Our Lord*, and *Jesus, Mary and Joseph*. However, Mexico's Jesus-centric films are mostly unknown outside of their home country.

The 1940s also saw the first feature-length theatrical American production of the sound film era that depicted Jesus Christ as a full-frontal walking, talking central character – in color, no less! But it was not made in Hollywood. Instead, it was shot in an Oklahoma site called Holy City of the Wichitas, located outside of the city of Lawton. In many ways, the back story on the film's creation is more fascinating than the on-screen presentation, although the film is not without its value.

In 1926, a Congregational minister named Rev. Anthony Mark Wallock originated the *Lawton Passion Play*, modeled after the famous production staged at Oberammergau, Germany. This annual event was staged at Eastertime in a natural amphitheater within a 150-acre property leased from the federal government, with non-professional actors from Lawton as the cast. The pageant was initially a modest affair, but over the years the size and scope of the effort swelled, and attendance grew into the tens of thousands. In 1934, the Works Progress Administration sent laborers to build the massive stone sets to be used for the Jerusalem setting of Passion Play. To be blunt, the sets bore little resemblance to architecture of ancient Judea, but at least there was a visual backdrop for the sequences set in the Garden of Gethsemane, Pilate's judgment hall, and Herod's Court.

In 1948, three oilmen from Tulsa created a company called Principle Films Inc. with the goal of making a filmed record of this endeavor. Harold Daniels, a one-time actor turned B-movie director, was recruited to run the behind-the-camera action. The wealthy trio from Tulsa gave Daniels a 16mm camera and a generous amount of Cinecolor film stock, plus enough funds to hire Hollywood cinematographer Henry Sharp, who lensed such classics as Douglas Fairbanks' *The Iron Mask* and the Marx Brothers' *Duck Soup*. Daniels and Sharp worked with the pageant actors and over a period of several months reportedly shot the entire four-hour event.

From here, the story becomes slightly bizarre. News of this production reached Kroger Babb, an exploitation film producer and distributor who scored a surprising box-office bonanza with *Mom and Dad*, a crudely made exploitation film about a young girl who finds herself with an unexpected pregnancy. Babb shrewdly recognized the commercial potential of a film on the life of Jesus – there was no Hollywood production on the subject since Cecil B. DeMille's *King of Kings* in 1927 – and he established a partnership between Principle Films and his Hallmark Productions.

Incredibly, Babb decided to jettison most of the footage shot by Daniels and Sharp and hired veteran filmmaker William Beaudine to craft new footage. Initially, the plan was to focus on the life of Rev. Wallock, played by longtime Western actor Forrest Taylor. But Babb instead spun a new tale that found the pious clergyman feuding with his unreligious brother (played by character actor Ferris Taylor, no relation to Forrest). The bad blood between the brothers would be cleaned up by Rev. Wallock's granddaughter, played by a six-year-old from Atlanta named Ginger Prince. Babb envisioned Prince as a successor to Shirley Temple and promoted her as "42 inches and 42 pounds of Southern Charm." To further enhance her cutesy persona, Babb gave her three songs to perform.

The first half of this new film, entitled *The Lawton Story*, focused on the musical melodrama with little Ginger and her dysfunctional clan. After an intermission, the film of the Oklahoma version of the Passion Play is presented.

So, what can we say about *The Lawton Story* as a seminal moment in Christian cinema? Well, it depends on the viewer's patience. In fairness, the play itself was never intended to be seen as a Broadway-worthy production, and the camera cruelly magnified the non-professional cast's shortcomings. Line readings are mostly delivered in a flat manner, with a heavy Oklahoma twang that gives Biblical dialogue an unusual country flavor, and a few crude special visual effects signifying holy happenings were haphazardly added in post-production.

The costuming is also quite a sight. If one accepts Biblical history from *The Lawton Story*, the Jerusalemites of Jesus' day wore vibrant pastel robes – except, of course, for Jesus (who dresses in white) and Judas (who is the man in black). The Three Kings were also a strange trio, with their paper crowns and Santa Claus beards, although the infant Jesus (played by the newborn son of one of the cast members) stole the Nativity scene with his natural charisma.

One of the most notorious aspects of *The Lawton Story* involves the procession to Calvary. The Holy City of the Wichitas is surrounded by poles and wiring that supplies power to the region. These modern-day structures are visible on screen, which creates a distracting anachronism during the film's greatest dramatic moments.

However, it is impossible to dislike *The Lawton Story*. The sincerity of the players shines from start to finish, and the utter lack of pretension reaffirms the genuine love of the subject carried by all involved. Millard Coody, a Lawton banker, was a physically commanding presence – a tall and thin man with a stern expression, he looked like an Eastern Orthodox icon come to life as he towered over those around him. And even with his Oklahoma drawl, his recitation of Jesus' teachings is presented with a sense of compassionate authority.

The Lawton Story premiered on April 1, 1949, at two theaters in Lawton and one in nearby Fort Still. Babb flew in a couple of minor Hollywood stars, comic Hugh Herbert and sexpot Lynn Bari, plus little Ginger Prince for the premiere. The audiences reportedly loved it.

But there was less love when Babb tried to take the film to other markets. The cast's Oklahoma accents created confusion and derision among audiences, and the title was meaningless to anyone outside of Lawton. Babb retitled the film *The Prince of Peace* and hired radio actors to dub the soundtrack. This version received a road show release that lasted years and became a financial hit; it even became a popular film in jaded New York City, much to Babb's happy surprise. However, critics expressed displeasure at Ginger Prince's treacly antics, preferring the story of Jesus to the would-be Shirley Temple.

After the theatrical run came to an end, Babb was supposed to transfer the rights to the film plus the original material to the Wichita Mountains Easter Pageant Association along with a $100,000 check. But Babb did not live up to his side of the agreement, and a lengthy legal battle transpired. Babb eventually sent the Passion Play portion of the film back to Oklahoma, but it was chopped into small pieces; the $100,000 was never transferred. Babb held the Ginger Prince footage, but it was never screened again and today it is considered lost.

Today, the only surviving copy of *The Lawton Story* runs 72 minutes and consists solely of a brief introduction of the players narrated by radio actor Knox Manning and the Passion Play itself. The surviving footage was painstakingly reassembled by Lewis T. Philips, a Florida man who learned of the film's fate and volunteered to put it back together. VHS video copies of the film were briefly on sale at a gift store in the Holy City of the Wichitas, but to date there has never been a proper DVD or Blu-ray release. *The Lawton Story* would occasionally be screened in Lawton at the historic Vaska Theater, delighting local audiences that participated in the production.

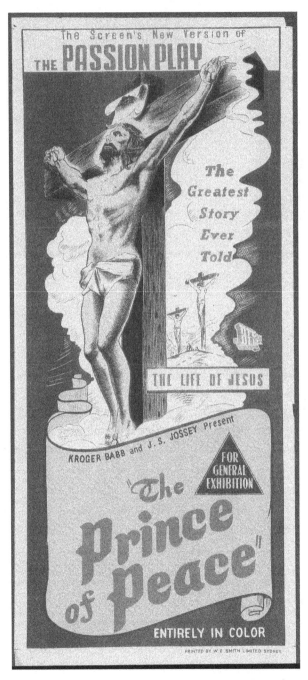

Poster art for the Australian release of the Oklahoma-lensed The Prince of Peace, originally distributed in the U.S. as The Lawton Story.

Chapter Three: Jesus on the Widescreen

"The signs of a true apostle were performed among you with utmost patience, with signs and wonders and mighty works."
– 2 Corinthians 12:12

The first Jesus film made in the 1950s was the British production *The Westminster Passion Play – Behold the Man*, which was released in 1951. As cited earlier, British censors decided that it would be inappropriate for films to offer a walking, talking, on-screen depiction of Jesus. This created a problem when the Roman Catholic organization Companions of the Cross wanted to create a film version of the play *Ecce Homo*, also known as the *Westminster Passion Play*, which was staged annually in London.

The producers and the censors reached a compromise by allowing the play to be adapted without the actors speaking lines. Instead, they would emote in pantomime while all the dialogue would be recited on the soundtrack by Walter Meyjes, the co-author of the play.

As you might imagine, having a silent film with a constant narration creates more problems than solutions – think of Charlie Chaplin's misguided 1942 re-release of *The Gold Rush*, with the funnyman giving a constant play-by-play on what was taking place in his silent classic. Mercifully, Meyjes' narration is less obnoxious than Chaplin's talkathon on *The Gold Rush* soundtrack. But even the most gifted orator would be hard pressed to breathe passion into the inert Passion Play put on the screen.

The Westminster Passion Play – Behold the Man appears to have been made on a tiny budget. This is obvious when the same barren and rocky hill top is used to stage Jesus' arrival in Jerusalem, the Garden of Gethsemane sequence, and the crucifixion at Golgotha. The film also keeps much of the unpleasant violence of Jesus' arrest and execution off-screen. Thus, the narration tells us of how the Roman soldiers beat and mocked Jesus while the on-screen action focuses on Pontius Pilate struggling with angst. And the Crucifixion only shows the base of the cross – there is no image of Jesus

Charles P. Carr as Jesus in the 1951 production The Westminster Passion Play – Behold the Man.

dying from the torture. The narrator also informs the viewer that Jesus was crucified between two criminals, but the on-screen image only shows one cross rather than three.

And then there is the problem of the film's pacing. This is, arguably, among the slowest moving films in cinema history. Director Walter Rilla, a German actor making his debut behind the camera, created a motion picture with minimal motion. This becomes acutely annoying when the characters are forced to react to the drama surrounding Jesus' final days – there is a surplus of widening eyes, clenched jaws, extended hands, upturned chins and stiffened shoulders, all executed in weirdly lethargic physical movements.

If there is one redeeming feature, it involves mini-eruptions of genius by Charles P. Carr as Jesus in two key segments: while praying in anguish at Gethsemane and struggling under the weight of the cross, the actor effectively captures the physical and emotional suffering of Jesus with a depth that is startling. But in the rest of the film, Carr moves and behaves in a robotic manner that makes him as detached from reality as the rest of his castmates.

The Westminster Passion Play – Behold the Man opened theatrically in London and received scathing reviews that called into question the deadly slow pace and the production's inability to transcend good intentions with good filmmaking. In 1954, the film turned up on the BBC as part of the network's Easter programming, and it became a staple of British television's Easter offerings during much of the 1950s. It did not play theatrically in the U.S., but a 65-minute version of the original 75-minute work was circulated in the nontheatrical market as *Behold the Man*.

In 1952, the first Asian film about the life of Jesus was created in the Philippines. *Kalbaryo ni Hesus* starred the American-born Jennings Sturgeon as Jesus and a cast of well-known Filipino actors under the direction of Carlos Vander Tolosa, a prolific filmmaker within the Manila-based film industry. The film was based on the dramatic reenactments of the Passion of Jesus that occur annually during Holy Week in the Philippines.

Kalbaryo ni Hesus was never released beyond its country and today it is primarily acknowledged in the wider span of cinematic scholarship as a historic footnote rather than a major step forward within this genre.

As mentioned earlier, Rev. James K. Friedrich followed the 1941 theatrical release of *The Great Commandment* by focusing the attention of his Cathedral Films production company on making short films for the non-theatrical market. In the 1950s, Cathedral Films branched out into television, creating the 12-part series *The Living Christ* and the one-hour 1953 film *I Beheld His Glory*. Texas-born actor Robert Wilson portrayed Jesus in these television works, which received positive response from viewers.

Empowered by this success on the small screen, Friedrich spun off a new entity called Century Films as the vehicle to bring his version of Christian filmmaking to the theatrical market. Friedrich unveiled his plan in a July 1952 interview with The *New York Times*, stating he "felt the need for a stronger spiritual counter-attack upon Communism in this country."

Century Films' 1954 *Day of Triumph* was shot in Eastmancolor at the Hal Roach Studio in Hollywood and included a couple of prominent actors to help bolster its box office appeal. However, the need for star power threw *Day of Triumph* somewhat out of kilter.

The core focus of the film is not Jesus, but a new character named Zadok, the leader of a brigade of zealots. Zadok was played by the prominent actor Lee J. Cobb, who received top billing; Robert Wilson's Jesus was second billed in the credits and had less screen time than Cobb's character.

Day of Triumph retells Jesus' life in recollections by Zadok of how his path crossed with the Nazarene, who is referred to as "Jesus Bar Joseph." Zadok also maintains relationships with Barabbas and future Disciples Simon and Andrew. The film eschews the Nativity and childhood years and presents the adult Jesus already into His ministry. Zadok and his fellow zealots, including a young Judas Iscariot, are an audience to John the Baptist's ranting against Herod and his subsequent arrest – oddly, Jesus and John do not meet in this film.

In the course of the plot, Zadok instructs Judas to go undercover among Jesus' followers and to report back on whether Jesus can be manipulated into becoming a zealot leader. When Jesus and Zadok finally meet during a dinner, Mary Magdalene abruptly shows up to clean Jesus' feet. Her appearance is utterly confusing, as one scene earlier she is depicted as a wealthy woman who is scornful of her maid's devotion to Jesus' teaching. Joanne Dru, a popular leading lady of the late 1940s, gives a strong presence that nearly compensates for the film's strange spin on the Gospels.

Even more curious is the depiction of Pilate's wife. Rather than have her briefly appear to warn her husband against prosecuting Jesus, she appears in an extended breakfast table conversation where she approves of Pilate's effort to shuck the legal responsibility of Jesus on Herod. Complicating matters, at least to a contemporary viewer, is the presence of then-unknown Barbara Billingsley as Pilate's wife – it is difficult to ignore how the future *Leave it to Beaver* matriarch brings a suburban American vibe to the court of Pilate.

The decision to shoot *Day of Judgement* in color was clearly a commercial choice since color films were mostly more popular with audiences in the 1950s than black-and-white alternatives. But the color cinematography also called great attention to this work's less-than-spectacular production values. (The film was reportedly made for $700,000, but it looks considerably cheaper.) Co-directors John T. Coyle (who helmed Cathedral Films' television work) and Irving Pichel (who directed the company's *The Great Commandment*) brought nothing in the way of visual style to the endeavor. Neither director seemed able to plumb a charismatic performance out of Robert Wilson, whose Jesus comes across as a stiff and slightly dull figure.

Day of Judgment was not a popular title in commercial release. It didn't help that start-up Century Films chose to self-distribute the film rather than hand it off to an established distribution company with a greater command of the market. As a result, its screen dates were scattered and limited, and most people would come to know *Day of Judgment* years later when it would become an Easter season staple on television. Friedrich would not make another feature-length film for theatrical release, focusing instead on short films for television and non-theatrical distribution.

Spanish filmmaker Ladislao Vajda brought an unexpected Jesus to the screen in the 1955 *Marcelino, pan y vino* (released in the U.S. as *Miracle of Marcelino*). This sweet feature film focused on a young orphan living in a monastery who discovers a statue of a crucified Jesus in an attic. Believing the statue is hungry, the boy spirits away bread and wine from the monastery's kitchen for the statue, who comes to life (albeit off-screen). For the benefit of those unfamiliar with the film and who abhor spoilers, it can be said the film's twist ending is thoroughly unexpected and deeply moving.

The Quasi-Jesus Epics

As the sound film era progressed, the major Hollywood studios seemed to lose interest in epic films with a Jesus connection. Metro-Goldwyn-Mayer had toyed with a remake of *Quo Vadis* in the late 1930s and even began scouting locations in Italy – but whether this was intended for second unit shooting or for an Italian-based primary production is unclear. World War II put that endeavor on hold, and the closure of the European theatrical market during wartime cancelled any consideration of extravagant Biblical epics that would have required global audiences to become a commercial success.

In 1948, MGM revived its efforts to produce *Quo Vadis* and leased the Cinecitta Studios outside of Rome for the production. Principal photography began with John Huston as the director, working under the supervision of producer Arthur Hornblow, with Gregory Peck and Elizabeth Taylor heading the cast. But MGM chief Louis B. Mayer was unhappy with the early footage that was sent from Rome and shut down the production. In 1950, production resumed with a new screenplay under the creative control of producer Sam Zimblast and director Mervyn LeRoy, with Robert Taylor and Deborah Kerr heading the cast.

The 1951 MGM presentation of *Quo Vadis* seemed to take its cue from the poorly-received 1925 Italian version of the Sienkiewicz epic by placing more focus on the visual spectacle of corrupt ancient Rome than the religious piety that Sienkiewicz envisioned in his text. Unlike the 1913 film version where Jesus makes a bold appearance at the end of the film, this production's Jesus is seen several times in the film in brief and fleeting moments - an opening sequence depicting the Crucifixion, and in segments when St. Peter recalls His ministry.

For most of these flashbacks, Jesus is viewed facing away from the camera, with his face out of sight. But in a very brief scene depicting the Last Supper – which was framed to replicate Leonardo da Vinci's landmark painting – Jesus is seen full-face. It is a startling moment, with a full-color, full-frontal Jesus in a Hollywood production. Unfortunately, it is over as quickly as it occurs and the actor assigned this role in *Quo Vadis* was not given screen credit.

Quo Vadis was a major commercial success, and the Hollywood studios began to review potential properties that involved some aspect of Jesus' life and ministry but without having Jesus as a front-and-center character. Columbia Pictures'1953 release *Salome* recalled the New Testament dance that resulted in the beheading of John the Baptist. Although the film bore absolutely no resemblance to anything found in the Gospels, leading lady Rita Hayworth looked great in revealing costumes and was electrifying in her climactic dance – which was followed by Salome giving up her sensual bump-and-grind talent to attend the Sermon on the Mount as presented by another off-screen Jesus.

Not to be outdone was 20th Century-Fox, which had acquired Lloyd C. Douglas' 1942 novel *The Robe* about a Roman military tribune who acquires the robe worn by Jesus on the day of the Crucifixion. The studio believed this property would offer the epic trappings needed to promote its investment in CinemaScope, an anamorphic widescreen process that was being positioned as the key to win audiences lured from cinemas by television – and was also being promoted as a cost-effective alternative to 3D films (with their bulky special glasses to perceive the screen's visual effects) and the complex Cinerama process that involved the simultaneous projection of three reels of film on a massively curved screen.

In *The Robe*, Jesus is never seen in a full-frontal manner, although He is given an off-screen voice dubbed in by Cameron Mitchell. Jesus' on-screen presence is relatively brief in the 135-minute film, but His impact drives the main characters of the tribune, Marcellus (played by Welsh actor Richard Burton in his first Hollywood starring role), the slave Demetrius (Victor Mature) and Marcellus' wife Diana (Jean Simmons). Marcellus wins Jesus' robe at Golgotha in a dice game, while Demetrius had previously seen Jesus arrive in Jerusalem and became obsessed with what he can gather about Jesus' teaching. Both men become Christians and Diana also accepts the new faith based on the Nazarene's ministry. None of this pleases the mad Emperor Caligula, who orders the executions of Marcellus and Diana; Demetrius escapes and winds up in the film's 1954 sequel *Demetrius and the Gladiators*.

The Robe is not a great film – the neuroses that burden the central characters as they transition from Roman paganism to Christianity is soapy and verbose, and the acting is all over the place, from Burton's histrionics to Mature's dull line readings. But the film offered great entertainment to audiences being introduced to the visual spectacle in the CinemaScope format. The critic for *Variety* summed up the reaction of the day: "It is a 'big' picture in every sense of the word. One magnificent scene after another, under the anamorphic technique, unveils the splendor that was Rome and the turbulence that was Jerusalem at the time of Christ on Calvary."

The Robe was a box office phenomenon and fed an audience interest in *Demetrius and the Gladiators*, which was produced in conjunction with *The Robe*. The second film puts too much emphasis on the gladiator aspect of the tale, with Victor Mature showing off his muscles rather than his dramatic skills. It also provides some distracting views of the machinations of Messalina, the wife of the Emperor Claudius who is played by Susan Hayward in a wardrobe that leaves nothing to the imagination. Whatever its deficits, audiences in 1954 didn't seem to mind as this offering – also shot in CinemaScope – reigned at the box office.

The one-two punch from these widescreen movies with a Biblical setting were commercial gold. Cecil B. DeMille got the message with his 1956 masterwork *The Ten Commandments*, albeit an Old Testament-focused production. While this version of *The Ten Commandments* was meant to one-up DeMille's 1923 silent version, the director never considered remaking his *King of Kings* – but before his death in 1959, he was considering a possible feature inspired by the Book of Revelation. Sadly, no one ever picked up the concept of that unmade work and brought it into fruition.

Metro-Goldwyn-Mayer sought to one-up DeMille by revisiting its silent epic *Ben-Hur*. Released in 1959, the production cost a massive (for the era) $15 million, and it seemed like every cent was represented on the screen: 300 sets, including an 18-acre arena used for the celebrated chariot race, and more than 10,000 extras captured in the vibrancy of 65mm Technicolor.

Following in the footsteps of the 1925 original, *Ben-Hur* opted not to provide a full-frontal view of Jesus. Instead, director William Wyler either photographed Him from behind, as an extended hand, or from a distance with His face down. Claude Heater, a six-foot-four American baritone who performed at many European opera houses, was cast as Jesus but was not given any dialogue or facial exposure. Ironically, Heater was cast after being recruited by production manager Henry Henigson, who praised Heater for his voice and appearance.

"Mainly, they were interested in hands," Heater recalled in a 1992 interview with the *Marin Independent Journal*, a California newspaper. "They wanted strong, but sensitive, hands."

Heater added that he must have made a positive impression, as "there were people on the set who would see me, drop to one knee and make the sign of Christ."

Indeed, much of the on-screen piety in *Ben-Hur* involves Charlton Heston (in the title role) and the other actors looking in awe at the mostly off-screen Heater and becoming humbled in the presence of this near-phantom presence. Not surprisingly, *Ben-Hur* is celebrated today for its spectacle rather than its spiritualism. The film was a box office bonanza and gained 12 Academy Award nominations while taking home 11 of the Oscar statuettes.

But not every epic of this era hit paydirt. Also in 1959 was a Jesus-inspired epic that became celebrated for the wrong reasons: *The Big Fisherman* was adapted from a Lloyd C. Douglas novel about St. Peter. The film had an intriguing parentage: Walt Disney Productions co-produced the feature and released it through its Buena Vista Distribution subsidiary, while veteran director Frank Borzage and longtime producer Rowland V. Lee helmed its creation. The role of St. Peter went to Howard Keel, a musical comedy star who transitioned to Biblical drama while wearing a rather elaborate wig and lush beard.

Unfortunately for the film, cinematographer Lee Garmes' 70mm camera captured a surprisingly high number of gaffes, including the presence of microphone booms and klieg lights and a highly visible vaccination mark on temptress Martha Hyer's bare arm. Jesus is a fleeting presence here, viewed by an outstretched hand and a dangling hem of robe.

At three hours in length, *The Big Fisherman* was mostly described by unimpressed critics as "plodding," and the film's commercial failure ensured the Disney organization would not create another Biblical epic.

The mania for mega-epics inspired by Jesus quieted until 1962 when Italian producer Dino De Laurenttis assembled an international cast for *Barabbas*, based on the novel by Nobel laureate Pär Lagerkvist. (An earlier film version of the book was released in Sweden in 1953, but it was not widely seen outside of its native country.) Anthony Quinn played the title role of the convicted thief who is released by Pontius Pilate in the place of Jesus. The Crucifixion is, arguably, the most striking visual presentation of Jesus' death ever captured on film, as director Richard Fleischer and cinematographer Aldo Tonti captured the segment during an actual solar eclipse that cast an eerie beauty on the most heartbreaking of tragedies.

Quinn's Barabbas is a remarkable character. He is initially scornful of Jesus' fate, but is impacted by both His death and the news of the Resurrection and begins to question his existence. Barabbas survives a second arrest, 20 years of enslavement in the Roman sulfur mines and grueling training as a gladiator. He comes to believe that he is doomed to live eternally because Jesus died in his place, and his belated embrace of Christianity during the great fire that destroys Rome brings him to a death by crucifixion where he fully embraces Jesus' mission and can exit the world in peace.

Roy Mangano, the brother of the film's leading lady Silvana Mangano and brother-in-law of De Laurentiis, is briefly seen in distant shots as Jesus. But the true glory here is Quinn's performance in the title role – unlike earlier and later cinematic depictions of Barabbas as a scowling but one-dimensional zealot, Quinn brings forth the emotional complexity of an unsophisticated man who is forced to process ideas and responsibilities beyond his comprehension. Unlike the other quasi-Jesus epics, *Barabbas* addresses questions of faith with maturity and innovative intelligence.

Outside of Hollywood, Europe's film industry churned out a number of cheap epics that used Jesus as a peripheral character on the edges of presentations that put more emphasis on style rather than substance. The 1958 *La Spade e La Croce*, released stateside in 1960 as *Mary Magdalene*, had Yvonne DeCarlo in the title role of a drama that reinvented the title character as the sister of Lazarus. The 1959 Spanish feature *Los Mysterios Del Rosario* crossed the Atlantic in 1965 as *The Redeemer* – it offered no famous stars and no full-frontal view of Jesus, whose back-to-the-camera presence was given an American voice dubbed by Macdonald Carey. The Italian effort *Ponzio Pilato* was filmed in 1961 with John Drew Barrymore as both Jesus (mostly obscured from view) and Judas, with an aged Basil Rathbone as Caiaphas, Jean Marais as Pilate and Jeanne Crain as Pilate's wife. European audiences didn't get to see this hodgepodge until 1964 and Americans had to wait until 1967. None of these dull films registered with critics or moviegoers and they deserve little acknowledgment beyond footnote status.

Jesus as a Heartthrob?

It was inevitable that Hollywood would eventually require a walking, talking Jesus who was fully on camera and a core character in the on-screen action. Metro-Goldwyn-Mayer made the first attempt to give audiences the first true Hollywood Jesus. Unfortunately, the studio's effort was not quite worthy of its lofty goals.

It is difficult to view the 1961 version of *King of Kings* without wondering whether the creative talent involved in the production had any familiarity with the inspiration for their work. Although it was not unusual for Biblical epics to take some fanciful liberties with the subject matter, rarely has the sacred text been so wildly rewritten.

King of Kings was pushed forward by Samuel Bronston, a Romanian-born independent producer who advocated the use of Francisco Franco's post-World War II Spain as a setting for Hollywood epics. The lower costs of producing large-scale films in Spain, coupled with Franco's happy cooperation in providing hordes of extras from his military forces, made the country an ideal location for creating cost-effective extravaganzas.

Bronston zeroed in on the life of Jesus for a film after Metro-Goldwyn-Mayer's 1959 commercial success with *Ben-Hur* – and the studio agreed to distribute Bronston's work, which carried a then-impressive $8 million budget. And although the film was shot in Spain, film historians have pegged it as the first sound-era Hollywood studio production to offer an on-screen Jesus as the central character of a film.

Oddly, Bronston picked Nicholas Ray to direct *King of Kings*. Ray excelled in moody melodramas such as *In a Lonely Place* (1950) and *Rebel Without a Cause* (1955) and in offbeat happenings including the brilliantly warped Joan Crawford Western *Johnny Guitar* (1954) and the Arctic adventure *The Savage Innocents* (1960) with the unlikely casting of Anthony Quinn as an Eskimo – which, of course, inspired Bob Dylan's ode to "Quinn the Eskimo" in his beloved song "The Mighty Quinn."

But Ray had no previous experience of being at the helm of a costume epic set in Biblical times, and his situation was not helped by casting of Jeffrey Hunter as Jesus. Hunter was a boyishly handsome, blue-eyed screen presence who gained a loyal following among young female moviegoers who were more enchanted with his physical beauty than his thespian skills. Although he was a capable actor when given the right material, most notably in his role opposite John Wayne in John Ford's classic *The Searchers* (1956), few people acknowledged him to be an actor of great dramatic range.

Hunter himself may have been confused on his casting, giving Hollywood gossip diva Louella Parsons the astonishing explanation, "Christ was a carpenter and 33 years old, and I am 33, and I suppose my physical measurements fitted the description in the New Testament. At the time of His death, He was robust, and not a delicate man."

Hunter was fitted with a reddish-blonde wig that looked conspicuously artificial and a red cloak that seemed a bit flashy for a poor carpenter from Nazareth. Hunter also shaved his body hair for Crucifixion because it did not match the color of his wig.

But the problems with Hunter were only obvious when he was on screen, which was not that often in *King of Kings*. Philip Yordan's screenplay assigned Jesus to a near-supporting role, with a mad mix of violent and off-kilter characters taking up much of the running time. Yordan opted to open the story decades ahead of the Nativity with Pompey's conquest of Jerusalem in 63 BC, which set the foundation for the sociopolitical circumstances in the period around Jesus' birth.

In *King of Kings*, the Nativity happens in a split-second – no sooner have Mary and Joseph entered the manger than the Three Wise Men show up. Identified by narrator Orson Welles by their folkloric (but non-Biblical) names of Melchior, Caspar and Balthazar, they arrive with ornate gifts, although Mary (played by the red-haired Irish theater star Siobhan McKenna) looks at their presentation with mild indifference. The lack of surprise follows Mary throughout *King of Kings* – further into the film, she is visited at home by John the Baptist and later by Mary Magdalene, and she acknowledges both guests with an air of vague resignation over her son's penchant for attracting scruffy friends.

Yordan's screenplay kicks around the Biblical facts with FIFA-worthy gusto, misidentifying Herod the Great as an Arab and having him order the Roman centurions to carry out the Massacre of the Innocents – never mind that the Roman legions would not have taken orders from a puppet king installed by Rome. Yordan also invented the character of Lucius, the centurion who coordinated the massacre and would later intersect with Jesus while taking the census in Nazareth when the Nazarene was 12. Lucius also turns up to serve as Jesus' legal advocate during the trial by Pontius Pilate. Herod's death in the film is sped up by a fatal action from his scheming son Herod Antipas (again, no historic record of that), and the film gives the impression that he inherited his father's entire realm, when Herod's kingdom was actually divided by Rome among his three sons.

The film also imagined Herod Antipas and his wife Herodias as having a chummy relationship with Pontius Pilate and his wife, who is called Claudia on-screen although she is not identified by name in the Gospel of Matthew, the only Biblical book that acknowledges her existence. The two couples hang out for dinner and conversation, occasionally joined by the high priest Caiaphas, who sourly reminds everyone that the people dislike the religious leaders of Judea because they were chosen by Rome. (The insertion of Caiaphas' observation comes from the 1st-century Jewish historian Josephus and not the Gospels.)

Herod Antipas, Pilate and Caiaphas keep a surveillance on John the Baptist – and, yes, Salome shows up for a Minsky-worthy dance that results in the baptizer's head on a silver platter, although Jesus makes a surprise visit to the dungeon to see John before his decapitating death. And, as luck would have it, Lucius the centurion is also running the dungeon and allows John to enjoy some quality time out of his chains.

But there is also Barabbas, who is leading his army of Jewish rebels against Rome. In the Gospel According to Yordan, Barabbas staged a brazen ambush on Pilate and then tried to stir an uprising in Jerusalem after Jesus enters the city riding on a donkey. Barabbas' second in command is Judas Iscariot, who was torn between Barabbas' muscular pushback against Rome and Jesus' pacifist teachings. And, yes, you know how this turns out – the film isn't *that* revisionist!

With all of these shenanigans going on, there is precious little time for Jesus. As a result, the bulk of His miracles and His teachings don't make it to the screen. The Sermon on the Mount does get a nice chunk of footage, with Jesus wandering through the masses while dropping his insights with a surprising degree of insouciance. Jeffrey Hunter's reedy voice fails to deliver the majesty of the sermon, and it is surprising that anyone outside of those standing three feet from Jesus could hear what is being said.

Oh, and narrator Orson Welles insists on using a hard "t" pronunciation of "apostle." Don't ask why.

King of Kings is certainly a big film, with tons of extras running about in various action sequences and overcrowding the spaces for Jesus' sermon. But producer Bronston failed to deliver on the level of star wattage that one associates with Biblical epics. Robert Ryan as John the Baptist was the biggest name of the bunch, with B-list-ers Hurd Hatfield, Rita Gam, Viveca Lindfors, Guy Rolfe and Ron Randell, along with then-up and coming actors Rip Torn (as the neurotic Judas Iscariot) and Harry Guardino (as the Brooklyn-accented Barabbas). Perhaps in gratitude for being able to shoot in Spain, Bronston cast Spanish stars Carmen Sevilla (as Mary Magdalene), Gerard Tichy (as Joseph), Antonio Mayans (as the apostle John) and Luis Prendes (as the penitent thief); the Spanish stars' lines were badly dubbed with voices that did not quite match their appearances.

Reviews of *King of Kings* were mixed to negative and the box office return was below what Bronston had anticipated. An unknown Hollywood smart-aleck dubbed the film "I Was a Teenage Jesus" because of Hunter's youthful appearance. But Hunter would claim in a 1964 interview with the *Chicago Tribune* that the film had a positive impact on many people.

"I still get an average of 1,500 letters a month from people who saw me in that film and share the beauty and inspiration I derived from it with me," Hunter said. "There are some things that can't be measured in dollars and cents and how can anyone put a price – even the price of a million-dollar career – on the role of the greatest Being this mortal world has ever known?"

Jesus in the Southwest

Of all of the films in the Jesus-focused cinema, *The Greatest Story Ever Told* had the longest production history. The work first appeared in 1947 as a half-hour weekly radio series written by playwright Henry Denker that ran for 10 years and won a special Peabody Award. In 1949, the series was adapted as a book by *Reader's Digest* editor Fulton Oursler. 20th Century- Fox acquired the screen rights to Oursler's book shortly before it was published and assigned screenwriter Philip Dunne to create a script; Dunne was also pegged to direct the film. However, Dunne felt overwhelmed by the project and withdrew, and it languished at the studio until 1958 when director George Stevens agreed to take on the work following the completion of his film version of *The Diary of Anne Frank*.

Stevens charged the studio a $1 million fee for his services, and then billed the studio for an extensive pre-production period. Stevens consulted with 36 Protestant leaders across the United States and later traveled overseas for meetings with Pope John XXIII in Rome and Prime Minister David Ben-Gurion in Israel to seek insight on the subject. He also commissioned French artist Andre Girard to create 352 oil paintings of New Testament scenes. Poet Carl Sandburg was recruited in a consulting role – he would receive an "In Creative Association with Carl Sandburg" acknowledgement in the opening titles – while screenwriter James Lee Barrett would share screenplay credit with Stevens.

Pre-production dragged on into the early 1960s before 20th Century-Fox pulled the plug – Stevens spent $2.3 million without shooting a single frame of film. Stevens successfully arranged to move the project to United Artists, which put up a $6 million budget.

Under the United Artists corporate banner, Stevens spent six weeks scouting out potential locations in Europe and the Middle East that could serve as the backdrop for his Biblical spectacle. Unhappy with what he found, Stevens made a bold and strange choice: he decided to shoot Jesus' life story in the American Southwest.

"I wanted to get an effect of grandeur as a background to Christ, and none of the Holy Land areas shape up with the excitement of the American southwest," he said. "I know that Colorado is not the Jordan, nor is Southern Utah Palestine. But our intention is to romanticize the area, and it can be done better here."

Yet Stevens failed to consider four significant problems. First, shooting an epic film in the United States was considerably more expensive than taking the production overseas. Second, the American Southwest did not look very much like the Holy Land – most notably in one scene where Jesus and the Disciples walk through a Judean village with a vast snow-covered mountain range hovering in the distance behind them.

The third problem involved choosing which format to use for cinematography. Stevens had originally planned to shoot his film in the three-camera Cinerama process that was introduced in a series of 1950s travelogues, starting with *This is Cinerama*, and later used in the all-star epics *The Wonderful World of the Brothers Grimm* and *How the West Was Won*. But 30 days into production, United Artists ordered Stevens to abandon the three-camera Cinerama process in favor of Ultra Panavision 70, which was being marketed as a single-camera Cinerama process because it matched the original's 2.76 aspect ratio without a three-camera projection set-up.

The fourth problem was the biggest: Stevens failed to consider that the American Southwest is not hot and sunny all year round. Production fell behind schedule due to the director's habit of shooting multiple takes and camera set-ups for even the most mundane of segments. Stevens was still shooting in Arizona in November and December of 1962 when the winter brought two snow storms that paralyzed production. David Sheiner, who was cast as James the Elder, would later recall the snowfall by wisecracking, "I thought we were shooting *Nanook of the North*." Unable to continue in the winter environment, Stevens moved the production to Hollywood and constructed a set resembling ancient Jerusalem that spread across a 40-acre lot.

Needless to say, the $6 million budget was quickly outgrown, and Stevens complicated matters with his insistence on multiple takes and a variety of camera set-ups on each scene. The initial three-month schedule stretched beyond nine months, which resulted in actors and crew being kept on payroll for much longer than originally planned. Some careless planning proved profitable to actor Sal Mineo, cast in a small role as a lame man healed by Jesus – his scenes were covered relatively quickly but he never received word that his work was finished and he wound up staying extra weeks on the Arizona location while collecting paychecks for no labor.

To his credit, Stevens realized that the central role of Jesus needed an actor who was not burdened with preconceived negativity by critics or audiences. His choice of the Swedish actor Max von Sydow to play Jesus was an unusually shrewd selection – critics appreciated his work in Ingmar Bergman's intense psychological dramas, but he was mostly unknown as a personality outside of his performances in those art house films. Also, his presence at the top of the cast would help in selling the film to the European market.

Stevens kept von Sydow from giving interviews during the production and would not release any publicity photos of the star prior to the film's opening.

Unfortunately, Stevens went to the other extreme in casting the rest of the film, with a surplus of highly recognizable actors crammed into a wide variety of roles. Too often, the film felt like an ecumenical version of all-star extravaganzas like *Around the World in 80 Days* or *It's a Mad, Mad, Mad, Mad World* that crammed so many stars into blink-and-you-miss-them moments. In this case, Shelley Winters turned up for a few seconds as an ill woman cured by touching Jesus' robe, Carroll Baker popped in and out as the apocryphal Veronica, Richard Conte scored a few seconds of screen time as a mute Barabbas released from prison and Pat Boone was barely on camera as the angel at the tomb.

Other big-name actors had more substantial parts, with varying degrees of subtlety: Claude Rains and Jose Ferrer were quietly malevolent as Herod the Great and Herod Antipas, but Charlton Heston bellowed his lines with outsized theatrical grandeur as John the Baptist. The mix of British and American actors offered a swirl of conflicting accents, most notably with Telly Savalas as the Long Island-accented Pontius Pilate and Angela Lansbury as his refined British-voiced wife. John Wayne's distinctive voice gave an Old West riff to his role as the centurion who looked upon the dead Christ – the iconic star, somewhat uncomfortably squeezed into his Roman costume, somberly declared in his husky Duke whisper, "Truly this man wuz the Son of Gawd." In contrast, Sidney Poitier was given no dialogue as Simon the Cyrene, but only looked on in mute anguish at the execution of Jesus.

But despite running wildly over budget and packing the film with too many prominent actors in too-small roles, *The Greatest Story Ever Told* resonated with power and intelligence. That's not to say it was a perfect work – there are points where the film is clumsily unsubtle, such as the initial appearance of Mary Magdalene (conflated with the woman accused of adultery) while wearing a bright scarlet robe and the blaring use of the "Hallelujah Chorus" from Handel's *Messiah* for both the raising of Lazarus and the realization of the Resurrection.

But Stevens made it clear from the beginning that his film would not be a rough-and-tumble affair epic along the lines of *Ben-Hur* or *King of Kings*.

"This will be a Biblical classic that has vigor in ideas, with no souped-up spectacles, no sword fights, no bacchanalian orgies," he stated in an interview ahead of the production, adding it would offer "the slightest narrative with no embellishments. The picture's significance will be in its words, its emotions and in the beauty and movement of its people."

Working on this principle, Stevens brought forth the most remarkable anomaly: an intellectual epic that carefully unfolded the power of Jesus' ministry. While detractors of the film complained that its pacing seemed enervated, Stevens was actually attempting to achieve a real-time presentation of how the ancient Judean world reacted to His presence. It was an intimate approach played out across a massive widescreen – something like this had never occurred before within the Hollywood Biblical epic genre, and it is not surprising that the experiment confused viewers who were expecting sword-and-sandal knockabout.

Perhaps the most effective aspect of *The Greatest Story Ever Told* involves Jesus' interaction with Satan during His 40 days and nights in the desert. Stevens has Jesus scaling a cliff and finding shelter in a cave, but this refuge was occupied by a scruffy old man (played by British actor Donald Pleasance) who is mildly eating the remains of some animal that he roasted on an open fire. At first, the elderly man (referred to in the film's press notes, if not in the actual film, as The Dark Hermit) seems like a benign if slightly eccentric presence. But then, the Dark Hermit begins to casually request the temptations: turning stone to bread, jumping from the great height with the expectation of angelic rescue and worshipping the satanic power to receive all of the kingdoms of the world. Stevens directed Pleasance to make these requests without any trace of *bwah-hah-hah* theatrical evil, but with the calmness of a grandfather asking a grandchild to close a window in order to stop a draft from blowing on him. In this sense, Stevens' Satan personifies Hannah Arendt's well-worn phrase of "the banality of evil" – and von Sydow's Jesus responds to these requests with a subtle mix of irritation at being audience to such malevolence with the physical anguish of a starving man who just climbed up the face of a cliff.

Pleasance's Dark Hermit returns later in the film, mingling with the crowds that surround Jesus during the growing popularity of His ministry. His deep black garment makes him stand out from earth tones favored by the Judean population, and his silent gaze at Jesus conducting His teachings grows more focused and agitated. He is also within the crowd when Pilate makes the public query on what should be Jesus' fate – here, the Dark Hermit is the first to yell "Crucify Him!", thus placing the sole blame for the deicide on Satan rather than the confused and fatigued Judean society.

Then, there is von Sydow's Jesus. Everything about the actor's presence makes him stand out from the others on the screen: his tall, gaunt physical presence gives the impression of an El Greco depiction of Jesus come to life, while his slightly accented voice does not fit into the jumble of British and American accents that populate the soundtrack. He speaks with a slow, thoughtful, almost elliptical deliberateness that is in contrast to the colloquial line readings of the other cast members. And in von Sydow's Jesus there is a constant sense of anguish that the actor projects through his body language – this Jesus appears to be carrying the weight of the world on His shoulders before He is forced to carry the cross.

Stevens made some adjustments to the Gospels for his screenplay: the unnamed rich young man is conflated with Lazarus – an understandable effort, if only to give Lazarus screen time ahead of his return from the dead. Judas does not hang himself after his betrayal, but instead does a free-fall into a burning sacrificial pyre in front of the Great Temple.

As for the production itself, *The Greatest Story Ever Told* wound up costing $20 million, making it both the most expensive Biblical film up to that time as well as the most expensive film shot exclusively in the United States. But, to use a corny cliché, every cent is up on the screen. The cinematography by William C. Mellor (who died of a heart attack midway through the production) and Loyal Griggs was among the most stunning of the 1960s widescreen cinema, and the recreation of Jerusalem was architecturally correct without falling victim to the florid embellishments of many

Biblical films. Some segments, such as the arrival of the Wise Men following the Star of Bethlehem and the sunrise over the lake on the morning of the Resurrection, were artistic triumphs staged and framed with a rare genius.

Whether the unevenness of *The Greatest Story Ever Told* veers to brilliance or disappointment has been a matter of personal taste. When first screened, the critics were split between admiring praise and snarky putdowns. Unfortunately for Stevens, United Artists quickly lost faith in the production and began to demand editing almost immediately after its first presentation. The original running time of 3 hours and 58 minutes was used for the U.S. road show release. For the British theatrical run, the footage was sliced down to 3 hours and 17 minutes, and then it was truncated to 2 hours and 17 minutes for the U.S. general release version. (Some sources claim that a version with a running time of 4 hours and 20 minutes was screened, but this may have been a director's cut assembled before the official theatrical release – there is no record of the film being shown at that considerable length.)

However, as the film was cut in length, acute damage was done to Stevens' careful planning – this was particularly problematic regarding Judas' character, who seems to lurk on the fringes of the shorter versions and acts with no clear delineation for his motives. The edited versions also created a rougher narrative flow that disrupted Stevens' vision. Ultimately, the shorter versions didn't help, as audiences by this time had been exhausted by Biblical epics for the past dozen years and were not in the mood for another. The poor box office returns on this film would discourage further Biblical epics for years to come.

Today, the 3-hour and 17-minute version of *The Greatest Story Ever Told* is available in the DVD and Blu-ray formats for home viewing and turns up occasionally on television. The original 3-hour and 58-minute version has not been restored for re-release.

Max Von Sydow as Jesus in George Stevens' The Greatest Story Ever Told *(1965).*

Chapter Four: A Different Jesus Emerges

"And while He was praying, the appearance of His face became
different, and His clothing became white and gleaming."
– Luke 9:29

Up until the 1960s, the cinema depiction of Jesus followed a consistent standard: the long-haired, bearded, white-robed figure of Renaissance paintings. The big screen Jesus was a symbol of piety and respect, with filmmakers and actors working within a clearly defined parameter.

But starting in the 1960s, things began to change. In many films, the on-screen Jesus began to take on appearances, clothing and a personality that were strikingly different from what came before. Some of this tinkering worked remarkably, while in many films the attempts at irreverence or edginess lapsed into vulgarity or puerility.

This notion of a different cinematic Jesus began with a short film that made relatively little impact in its day and is mostly unknown at this late date: The 1961 production *The Sin of Jesus*, directed by the Swiss-born Robert Frank and made on a farm in New Brunswick, New Jersey.

Based on the short story by the Russian writer Isaac Babel, *The Sin of Jesus* focused on a pregnant laborer at an isolated poultry farm. Her work is dreary and monotonous, and she goes through her days with a robotic indifference to her duties. When her indifferent boyfriend decides to leave her, she kneels in prayer and is visited by Jesus. And while the woman recognizes Jesus, the audience may not: he is presented with short hair and a clean-shaven face, and he wears a contemporary-style tunic and dark pants.

Jesus offers the woman an angel named Alfred as a mate – Alfred is unhappy being an angel and wants to return to Earth. Jesus tells the woman that she must remove Alfred's wings at night before he goes to sleep, otherwise he will die. On their wedding night, the woman and her angelic new husband indulge in a private celebration with cake and champagne. Alas, she neglects to follow instructions and awakes in the morning to find only Alfred's wings. She

Enrique Irazoqui as Jesus in Pier Paolo Pasolini's 1964 The Gospel According to St. Matthew.

carries them across the bleak rural landscape, weeping in remorse. Jesus appears and is not sympathetic to her plight. But when she continues mourning her loss, Jesus appears again to admit He was in error regarding His attitude to her and kneels to gain her forgiveness, which she bitterly withholds.

On its own terms, *The Sin of Jesus* is a poorly made film. Frank's previous film experience was the 1959 short romp *Pull My Daisy*, made in collaboration with Jack Kerouac, and the scruffy nature of that work mirrored the playful iconoclastic personalities of the Beat literary figures who turned up on the screen. However, *The Sin of Jesus* was meant to be a profound work, but the result included badly framed scenes with inadequate sound usage. The acting by Julie Bavasso as the severely unlucky woman and a young Telly Savalas as the man who leaves her gave the impression of acting students trying too hard to pass an audition.

But where *The Sin of Jesus* resonates is Roberts Blossom's Jesus. There is nothing holy about his demeanor – he is pensive and a bit annoyed at having to answer the woman's prayer. He speaks to the woman like an indifferent teacher rather than as a source of healing inspiration, and this Jesus presides over the wedding ceremony (populated by actors wearing cheap angel costumes and tossing feathers instead of rice or confetti) with no degree of emotional connection. His change of mind at the end and the genuflection before the woman is startling – this is the first time in film history that Jesus behaves like a humble man.

However, most people back in 1961 were not aware this film existed. Outside of a few screenings at film societies and venues specializing in underground short films, *The Sin of Jesus* was unknown to the wider world. Today, it is only called up as part of Frank's uneven and idiosyncratic film output, which includes the 1969 feature *Me and My Brother* plus a 1972 documentary on the Rolling Stones with a scatological title that prevented it from gaining wide exhibition.

Jesus at the World's Fair

In 1964, the most controversial movie playing in New York was not on the screen at some fleapit venue specializing in underground flicks, nor was it in the ritzy first-run houses that framed Times

Square. Instead, it was playing at the Protestant and Orthodox Center at the 1964/65 World's Fair. The film in question was called *Parable*, and the brouhaha surrounding its contents was nothing short of astonishing.

The Protestant and Orthodox Center was a World's Fair pavilion sponsored by the Protestant Council of New York City. More than 20 denominations were represented at this venue, which included a chapel, a children's center, and the "Court of Christian Pioneers" that honored the ministries of 34 notable theologians.

And while it may seem a bit odd to some contemporary readers that a religious pavilion would be part of a World's Fair, it should be noted that there were several faith-based venues at that event, including venues sponsored by the Mormons, the Christian Science faith, and the Roman Catholic Church – the latter represented by the Vatican's very popular pavilion that housed Michelangelo's "Pieta" in its first-ever presentation outside of Rome.

As with many World's Fair pavilions, the Protestant and Orthodox Center included a cinema that offered a special film created for the fair. But anyone that came to the center expecting a stodgy sermon-type offering was in for a shock because *Parable* took the message of Christ's teachings into a bold and surreal new realm.

Parable takes place in a traveling circus, and the film opens with the procession of animals and acrobats on their way to a new town. Trailing slightly behind the procession is a clown with a chalk-white head and face and an oversized white costume. The clown is riding a donkey, and whether he is part of the circus or just trailing along is not immediately clear.

The clown makes his way through the circus, gently interrupting the lives of several people. He takes buckets that an animal trainer has filled with lake water and brings it to a pair of elephants, and the parched pachyderms happily drink to quench their thirst. He then spies a dunk tank game where a white man in a suit is trying (and repeatedly) failing to submerge the black man sitting at the edge of the tank. The clown trades places with the black man – and when the white man throws a ball directly at the black man, it is caught and then tossed back to the would-be pitcher. A stray pitch winds up dunking the clown in the tank, but he emerges without smeared make-up.

The clown, followed by the animal trainer and dunk tank man, then breezes past a barker trying to sell tickets to a side show. The clown views an unhappy woman that is part of a magic act – he trades places with her, allowing her to escape from her position. (The speed of her exit suggests that her unhappiness is more than a mere case of being occupationally dissatisfied.)

The clown then enters the main circus tent, where Magnus the Great is performing his Living Marionettes act. This consists of three people strung up on harnesses above the audience, with Magnus sitting on a large throne while manipulating the cables that hold up his "living marionettes." The clown distracts the all-child audience by cleaning their feet with a whisk broom – and within seconds, all of the kids are cleaning the shoes of their peers. The clown pulls down the living marionettes, and they promptly slip out of their harnesses and run off – with the audience following them.

The clown then voluntarily puts himself into an empty harness, and Magnus hoists him into the air. The three men who had their day disrupted – the man throwing balls at the dunk tank, the barker and the man whose lady ran away from their magic act – come in and start to beat the clown. The magic act character takes a sword and stabs the clown, who is then hoisted higher. The clown cries in anguish and dies, suspended in midair.

Eventually, the circus folds up and rolls off to another town. But Magnus, who is guilt-ridden over what transpires, smears white make-up over his face and assumes the dead clown's costume – and he is last seen riding on the clown's donkey after the circus procession.

Directed by Rolf Forsberg and Tom Rook, based on Forsberg's dialogue-free screenplay, *Parable* offered a strange twist on the very familiar story of the Gospels. Several stories from Christ's life received an odd updating – for example, cleaning feet with whisk brooms instead of washing the feet – and there was also a very contemporary (if not very subtle) plea for racial equality in the ball toss at the dunk tank.

But the idea of a Christ-like figure in clown's make-up and costume was a wild artistic leap, and one that nearly killed *Parable* before it was screened. Somehow or other, word got out to Robert Moses, the president of the World's Fair, who imagined the worst – perhaps he thought the film would take an Emmett Kelly approach to clowning and have Jesus sweeping a spotlight with a broom. Moses put heavy pressure on the Protestant and Orthodox Center to withdraw the film. An executive with Con Edison, the local electrical utility, threatened to shut off power to that pavilion, and a local minister promised to take a gun to the pavilion and blast holes in the screen.

These protests only served to call attention to the film, and *Parable* quickly became a must-see attraction. To the shock of the film's detractors, it received rapturous praise from critics – *Newsweek* said it was "very probably the best film at the fair" – and the pavilion's 370-seat cinema was always filled to capacity.

After the World's Fair closed, *Parable* found its way into several major film festivals and into the film projectors at many churches and libraries. Although some controversy continued to shadow it – an attempt was made to have it purged from the Los Angeles public library's film collection in 1975 – *Parable* had a long life in non-theatrical release. However, co-director Forsberg would later complain that the non-theatrical settings were inappropriate to his visit – *Parable* was originally projected in a widescreen format, and Forsberg felt the production was poorly served in 16mm presentations. *Parable* had brief moment of late attention in 2012 when it was added to the Library of Congress' National Film Registry, and it later found its way into DVD release.

Elsewhere at the New York World's Fair was the Billy Graham Pavilion, sponsored by the evangelical leader's ministry. Graham's film operation, World Wide Picture Company, created *Man in the 5th Dimension*, a 28-minute nonfiction film to be shown to pavilion audiences in a specially constructed theater seating 400 people – each seat had an ear piece that enabled audience members to switch away from the English-language soundtrack in favor of a narration translated into either French, Spanish, Chinese, Russian, Japanese or German.

Even more remarkable was the decision to produce and exhibit the film in Todd-AO, a 70mm widescreen process that was used for major Hollywood epics such as *Around the World in 80 Days, The Alamo* and *Cleopatra.* Unlike those cinematic extravaganzas, *Man in the 5th Dimension* was primarily a one-person film, with Graham occupying most of the running time as either an on-camera host or a soundtrack narrator.

Man in the 5th Dimension opens with Graham standing before California's Palomar Observatory, describing the work that astronomers undertake in charting the vastness of the universe, with multiple galaxies millions of light years away from Earth. "Many of these astronomers believe that all of these galaxies are the same age, and they all started from the same place at the same time," Graham tells the viewer. Graham notes the opening sentence of the Bible, with God creating the heavens and Earth.

But then, Graham take an interesting turn, moving into a laboratory setting and commenting, "The Bible never tries to prove the existence of God, it assumes it. The problem is, too often, man tries to subject God to the analysis of the laboratory. We cannot put God in a test tube and say 'This is God,' no more than we can put a mother's love in a test tube and say, 'This is a mother's love.'"

Graham pauses before adding, "Of course, the evidences of God are all about us." He takes another turn into a consideration of miniscule organisms visible only under the most sophisticated microscopes, detouring again into a consideration of optic nerves within the human eye. "What more eloquent evidence of the creator's hand?" Graham asks. "No wonder so many of our scientists say there must be a God."

Graham asserts evidence of God existing through human morality. "We know it is wrong to murder, but how do we know?" he says. "It is the God-given voice of conscience within."

Graham offers an overview of God's personality and focus on love. The film switches to a redwood forest to discuss the Edenic rupture that resulted in the special bond between man and God. "And as God warned Adam, the penalty of sin is suffering and death," Graham intones.

Graham then starts to subtly guide the viewer into the central focus of this cinematic sermon, questioning God's dilemma over "how He could forgive man unless the penalty of sin had been paid." The solution, according to Graham: "God decided to become a man in the person of his son."

The film switches to the then-contemporary Holy Land, with Graham speeding through the Nativity Jesus' years in carpentry – a young man working in a carpenter's shop is depicted during this stretch of the narration – and then the camera roams through the Judean ruins as Graham reads on the soundtrack from several of Jesus' teachings. But Graham takes another unexpected turn in acknowledging the doubters in his audience. "To those who consider His words and study his life, one would conclude that either He was an egomaniac or a deliberate liar and deceiver of the people – or, He was who He claimed to be," he intones.

From here, the film takes on a travelogue aspect, with vast views of the Holy Land beautifully captured in the glory of the widescreen Todd-AO process as Graham continues with his overview of Jesus' ministry. But as the Christ story veers toward its Calvary climax, *Man in the 5th Dimension* offers its first and only depiction of Jesus via artistic interpretations of the Crucifixion. Jesus' face in not seen – the Crucifixion is depicted from a point of view focus fixed above and behind the cross, with the observers to His death looking upward in anguish at his slow and torturous death.

"What happened on that cross is a mystery," Graham says. "In some mysterious way, God took all of our sins and laid them on His son. God was saying from the cross to the whole human race: I love you. I will forgive you."

The film takes a quick history consideration of the spread of Christianity across the ancient world. Graham then takes the viewer into a setting designed to be a pantheon of great thought leaders, who are depicted in plaster busts on pedestals. Graham points out some of history's most influential individuals – including St. Augustine, Blaise Pascal, Leo Tolstoy, George Washington and Benjamin Franklin. To his credit, Graham doesn't sugarcoat American history. "Certainly not all of our forefathers were true believers," he admits. "There were many dark spots in America's early years – for example, slavery."

Graham then questions the relevance of the Bible and Jesus' ministry in the modern age. The film offers a line-up of impressive figures

– the dean of arts and sciences at George Washington University, the president of RCA and the senior staff psychiatrist of Harvard University – affirm Graham's vision. Thus, it would seem that leaders in education, commerce and psychiatry voice their support that Christ's message retains its relevancy.

Graham wraps the film by inviting the audience to meet with members of his ministry's staff in a section of the pavilion called the "counseling area," adding that "we'll only keep you for a few moments to give you literature and have prayer with you." The closing image is an intertitle that proclaims, "Jesus said, "I am the way, the truth and the life."

Man in the 5th Dimension played in 12 screenings per day during the World's Fair's two-year run, which required 11 Todd-AO prints being struck to accommodate the continuous presentations. Sadly, none of these 70mm prints survive, and *Man in the 5th Dimension* only exists today in the 16mm format. Edited versions were released in the non-theatrical market and have also surfaced on both the Billy Graham Evangelical Association's website and in an unauthorized posting on YouTube.

In many ways, *Parable* and *Man in the 5th Dimension* complement each other by taking very different approaches to the non-traditional retelling of the familiar story of Christ's work. *Parable* forces the viewer to remember and reconsider Jesus' life and death through an experimental artistic spectrum, while Graham's presentation is an intellectual challenge to a secular mindset. In some ways, his approach is more subversive by openly going into the secular shrines of science and citing leaders of education, business and psychiatry to unapologetically admit that their respective pursuits do not offer alternatives to the message that Jesus gave to the world. The absence of a physical Jesus is not detrimental to the film's power – in fact, having an actor pretending to be Jesus would have diluted the cerebral argument put forward by Graham.

Furthermore, the decision to put this presentation on the massive Todd-AO screen further reinforces Graham's boldness – what could have been an intimate and low-keyed lecture was presented to the World's Fair audiences as a complex challenge that could only be framed on a larger-than-life screen. As a narrator, Graham never raises his voice or berates the perceived skeptics of Jesus' message. His approach is serious but never pedantic, and his charismatic eloquence makes *Man in the 5th Dimension* a persuasive invitation to further explore the beauty of the Gospels.

The Neo-Realist Jesus

In 1962, the Italian filmmaker Pier Paolo Pasolini presented *La Ricotta*, a short film for inclusion in the omnibus feature *Ro. Go. Pa. G.* The film offered a funny-nasty story of a starving actor who is contracted to play one of the thieves crucified alongside Jesus at Calvary. The actor, after several attempts to secure a meal, overindulges on ricotta cheese left over from the film production company's catering table. But while strapped to the cross, the actor experiences severe gastric indigestion and abruptly dies – unbeknown to the film crew, who only discover his demise when the director (played by Orson Welles) yells "Action!" and gets no response from the now-deceased performer.

The Italian government took an unhappy view of Pasolini's work and he was accused of holding the state religion in contempt. A court sentenced him to four months in prison, but he avoided incarceration and paid a fine; an appeals court later voided the original conviction.

Pasolini was an atheist, Communist and homosexual. Despite the controversy surrounding *La Ricotta* and his conspicuous lack of public-facing piety, he was invited by Pope John XXIII to attend a conference in Assisi on how contemporary artists were depicting Jesus and the Bible. But the beloved pope's presence in Assisi created massive traffic jams that prevented Pasolini from reaching the Franciscan monastery where the conference was scheduled to take place. Instead, the filmmaker stayed in his hotel and picked up the copy of the Bible left in his room. Pasolini later claimed that he read the four Gospels in a single sitting and decided after his reading to pursue a film about Jesus. As he later recalled, the experience "threw in the shade all the other ideas for work I had in my head."

Pasolini created a film focused film entirely on a single Gospel – in this case, Matthew's version of the life of Jesus – rather than combine the four Gospels into a biographical presentation. By rooting his endeavor on Matthew's version, Pasolini's film omitted many of the incidents and characters that populated earlier Jesus-focused films, most notably Mary Magdalene.

Pasolini also took the artistic strategy to shoot his film in a Neo-Realist style. Stark, documentary-style black-and-white cinematography was employed instead of widescreen color, and ramshackle villages in southern Italy were used for the Judean locations. (Pasolini briefly considered filming in Israel, but found the country too modernized for his purposes.) He also decided to employ non-professionals for his cast, with the central role of Jesus bestowed on Enrique Irazoqui, a 19-year-old Spanish economics student. (Italian actor Enrico Maria Salerno was used to dub Irazoqui's dialogue for the Italian-language presentation.)

The resulting film was, quite frankly, unlike anything that ever came before it. Pasolini's *Il vangelo secondo Matteo* (known in English as *The Gospel According to St. Matthew* – the honorific sainthood was inserted against Pasolini's wishes) was a boldly iconoclastic version of the oft-told story. The grandeur and spectacle of Biblical epics was jettisoned in favor of a gritty, earthy and sometimes perplexing realignment of the sacred text. Veering closer to humanism than dogmatic Catholicism, Pasolini gave moviegoers a zealot Jesus bringing an extraordinary message to an intellectually and economically impoverished society.

For his soundtrack, Pasolini grabbed classical music selections plus eclectic pieces of 20th century African and African-American religious music – the result places familiar musical pieces in unfamiliar and unlikely physical settings, a technique that Stanley Kubrick would employ in his 1968 masterpiece *2001: A Space Odyssey*. Pasolini adapted his dialogue strictly from Matthew's Gospel, with no new lines added to the presentation. Some sources claim the film was made without a written screenplay, though it seems unlikely that Pasolini would have undertaken such an endeavor without clearly conceived notes.

From the opening sequence, Pasolini creates a very different foundation: the young Mary is seen in close-up, gazing with an enigmatic expression. The camera cuts to Joseph, who is visibly older than Mary and who gazes back at her with incredulity. The camera cuts back to Mary, who is now seen in full figure and conspicuously pregnant – yet she stares at Joseph with an unapologetic expression. The camera returns to Joseph, whose expression betrays a bafflement of events that do not require deciphering with endless dialogue.

Joseph storms off and falls asleep along the road, but is awakened by an angel who is depicted as a teenage girl with unruly dark hair. The angel proclaims the miracle of Mary's condition, which convinces Joseph to accept his role in circumstances beyond his control.

Pasolini stages the Nativity in a cave, and the visit of the Wise Men is offered without pomp and circumstance. Instead, three elderly men clothed in garments that define genteel shabby arrive to present their offerings to the newborn. The young angel warns Joseph to flee into Egypt, and Bethlehem is besieged by the assassination of the newborns while the soundtrack swells to Prokofiev's cantata from *Alexander Nevsky*. The angel returns later to signal the safety in Judea, and by now Joseph is the loving father of the toddler Jesus.

The film fast-forwards to Jesus' appearance before John the Baptist, who is presented with a lot less melodramatic emoting than in the Hollywood epics. Jesus is also significantly different from earlier cinematic interpretations: with his short, dark, slicked-back hair, unibrow and scruffy facial hair that barely qualifies as a mustache and beard, he looks nothing like the ethereal figure of religious art. Satan comes to Jesus in the guise of an average-looking man, and a humorless Jesus abruptly dismisses Satan's relatively uninspired temptations with indifference.

Jesus' miracles are presented in a matter-of-fact manner, with direct cuts transitioning the before- and after-effects of healing the leper and feeding the multitudes. Jesus' walking on water is shot at a great distance – obviously to hide the special effects for the segment, but also to recreate the space that a shore-bound viewer would have when viewing the aquatic scene.

John the Baptist's fate is presented in a rather startling manner when compared to earlier films. Imprisoned in Herod Antipas' dungeon, he wastes away in the darkness. Herod's stepdaughter Salome is first seen as a somewhat awkward early teen playing jacks by herself. Dressed by her mother in a rather modest outfit with a floral head-dress, she dances for the king in a completely inoffensive manner – far removed from the carnal gyrations of earlier movie depictions of Salome. When asked by the king for the reward for her dance, she provides an unemotional request for John the Baptist's head. In many ways, this is more shocking than the titillating Rita Hay-worth-level Salome driving themselves to choreographed states of near-orgasm – this young person's seemingly innocent dance makes her homicidal demand all the more unexpectedly stunning.

Sadly, the film's second half occasionally drags when Jesus arrives in Jerusalem – a mountain village poorly standing in for the great city – and engages in lengthy debates with the Pharisees and seem-ingly endless diatribes against the locals for going astray from God's word. Pasolini stages these dialogue-heavy scenes with static cam-erawork, creating a visually dull presentation of Jesus' intellectual assault on the faith leaders.

Also, the Passion is strangely limited here – the Pharisees are more intellectually bored than spiritually threatened by Jesus, the character of Pilate is on screen for roughly one minute, and Jesus barely suffers on the road to Calvary. Jesus' death on the cross is intercut with the destruction of an old building – the shaking of the camera is meant to suggest an earthquake. But the film ends on a powerful note when the tomb's stone falls on its own accord to a blast of the Congolese gloria from "Missa Luba" as the angel returns to declare Jesus' triumph over death. The crowd that learns of what transpired race to the hillside where the resurrected Jesus offers His final earthly message ahead of the Ascension.

To be blunt, Irazoqui's Jesus could easily be the least likable Jesus in film history. Often hostile and surly – he angrily berates those who come to arrest him at Gethsemane – this is a too-human Jesus who does not suffer fools lightly. And while Irazoqui was the youngest actor to play the role, he brings a somber maturity that far outweighs those around him. But outside of the anguished emot-ing of the director's mother Susanna Pasolini as Jesus' mother, no one but Irazoqui gives an in-depth performance. Instead, Pasolini mostly has his nonprofessional cast staring at Jesus and each other before speaking with minimal dialogue.

The Gospel According to St. Matthew was first screened in 1964 at the Venice Film Festival, where it won the OCIC Award and the Special Jury Prize. However, a U.S. theatrical release was not immediate – the commercial failure of *The Greatest Story Ever Told* after a glut of Biblical films, coupled with Pasolini's unusual approach to the subject, kept it out of U.S. theaters until Continental Distributing took the risk of bringing it across the Atlantic in 1966. The fears that Pasolini's work would not play in the U.S. were unfounded, as *The Gospel According to St. Matthew* was a critical and commercial success and received three Academy Award nominations.

The Silly Jesus

Among the major filmmakers of the post-World War II era, Luis Buñuel was particularly sharp in using cinema to poke fun at and openly question Christianity, particularly the Roman Catholic brand of the faith. Films such as *Nazarin* (1959), *Viridiana* (1961) and *Simon of the Desert* (1965) satirically questioned the dogma and protocol of the faith, with enough intelligent wit to keep Buñuel's criticism from spilling into offensive blasphemy. But, then again, Buñuel never intended malice in his mischief – after all, his most famous quote on the subject was "Thank God I'm an atheist."

Buñuel had included a Jesus lookalike in his controversial 1930 experimental film *L'age d'Or* – the character was actually inspired by the Duc de Blangis from the Marquis de Sade's *The 120 Days of Sodom*. In the great director's 1969 comedy *The Milky Way*, Jesus became a part of plot. But, strangely, Buñuel was not willing to extend his humor to Jesus – indeed, Jesus was the only major character in the film who was not given any funny lines.

The plot of *The Milky Way* involves a pair of French travelers who are journeying by foot from Paris to Santiago de Compostela in Spain's Galicia region, where they plan to visit the cathedral reportedly housing the Remains of St. James. The travelers find themselves in a series of surreal non-sequitur segments that call into question Catholic dogma and Christian history, as well as the pretensions and rudeness of those who claim to be devout students of Jesus' teaching. One lengthy sequence involves the maître 'd of a swank restaurant who lectures his staff on the importance of Christian brotherhood and charity, but who abruptly fails to practice what he preaches and shoos away the two French travelers when they make a raggedy appearance at his establishment. A more jolting sequence involves a nun who blithely allows her fellow sisters to perform a crucifixion by nailing her to a cross – the serenity of the tortured nun is astonishing when considering the mayhem that surrounds the reaction by a local priest.

Buñuel also engages in non-linear storytelling that enables the travelers to bear witness to a duel taking place two centuries earlier. There are some historical flashbacks, and that's where Jesus first comes in. When one traveler remarks about beards, the viewer is taken back to ancient Nazareth where the adult Jesus (played by French actor Bernard Verley) is preparing a cup full of shaving cream while studying his chin in a mirror. Jesus' mother Mary calmly informs Him that the beard aids His physical appearance, and Mary's recommendation is enough to make Jesus put down the shaving cup and forget about running a razor across His chin.

Later in the film, Jesus is back in a recreation of the Wedding at Cana – the only strange aspect is that He and the Disciples are late to the ceremony and need to move in a hurry. At the wedding, Jesus offers a too-serious telling of the Parable of the Unjust Steward, even though that parable belonged elsewhere in the Gospels. The actual changing of water into wine is not presented, leaving one to contemplate whether Buñuel intentionally left it out to question the veracity of Jesus' ability to work miracles or whether he could not come up with a suitable blackout gag for the scene.

Jesus and the Disciples turn up at the film's conclusion, where the travelers are joined by a harlot they met along the way and two blind men following Jesus. While Jesus appears to heal the blind men, they still rely on their canes to navigate the unfamiliar terrain. Again, the meaning of this can be open to debate.

"The Milky Way is neither for nor against anything at all," Buñuel would later write. "The film is above all a journey through fanaticism, where each person obstinately clings to his own particle of truth, ready, if need be, to kill or to die for it. The road traveled by the two pilgrims can represent, finally, any political or even aesthetic ideology."

Buñuel would also insist that his vision of Jesus was framed in a manner to show Him "as an ordinary man, laughing, running, mistaking his way, preparing to shave – to show, in other words, all those aspects completely alien to our traditional iconography." Yet in emphasizing His humanness, Buñuel offered a somewhat banal and unmemorable Jesus. The filmmaker may have realized that mistake – after all, he cast himself in the film as a pope being assassinated by revolutionaries, which is a much briefer yet much funnier role than the one written for the character of Jesus.

As the first comedy film to incorporate Jesus into its story, *The Milky Way* is relatively mild in its digs at the holy subject. Within Buñuel's canon, the film is considered by most critics as an entertaining but relatively minor endeavor. Within Jesus-focused cinema, it is a first blip of happy irreverence to the sacred subject.

In 1970, Baltimore-based underground filmmaker John Waters gave two versions of Jesus in his rowdy comedy feature *Multiple Maniacs*. The first version is a cute little boy dressed up as the living version of the statue of the Infant Jesus of Prague who leads Divine to a church, where the cross-dressing star has a sexual encounter with a strange woman played by Mink Stole. The tryst, which includes a rosary used in manner for which it was never intended, is juxtaposed against a dramatic recreation of the Stations of the Cross. In this second version of Jesus, Waters framed the Stations of the Cross sequence in a straightforward (albeit microbudget shabby) manner, with George Figgs playing the role in complete seriousness. As with Buñuel, the always outrageous Waters drew the line when it came to making Jesus a figure of fun.

Then there was the case of another underground film made in 1971 by Detroit-area neophyte filmmaker Peter McWilliams (working under the pseudonym Peter Alexander) that was shot under the working title *The Greatest Story Overtold* but later released in 1974 as *The Divine Mr. J.*

This work opens in Heaven, although it looks like a rather commonplace public garden. The film's on-screen narrator is the Angel

Fred, a deadpan character who explains that he wound up in Heaven following a fatal motorcycle accident. Angel Fred has a conversation with God, played by McWilliams doing a Harpo Marx imitation, and he explains that a film on Jesus' life has been made. God is initially unhappy that He has a tiny role but agrees to appear in the opening credits that spoofs the MGM titles by roaring like a lion under the banner "Metro Golda Meir."

This retelling of the sacred story takes place in a modern setting and is put into motion when a rabbi named Gabriel tricks a virgin named Mary that she is an angel sent by God to carry the deity's child. Mary isn't the brightest crayon in the box – she reads the National Enquirer, believes God is a woman and later naively explains to her husband Joseph how Gabriel collects money from other "angels" to have sex with her. Joseph, an incompetent would-be inventor, doesn't seem concerned with Mary's carnal activities. When trying to come up with a name for the child, Joseph accidentally slams his hand in a desk and curses aloud "Jesus Christ" – to which Mary declares that is a perfect name. Yes, that is the kind of humor on display here.

The film pinballs across the life of Jesus with unsubtle jokes, dropping references to the reign of "Herod Antipasto" and replacing the Three Kings with a trio of ridiculously effeminate men referred to as "queens" – and instead of gold, frankincense and myrrh, the baby Jesus is given a sled with "Rosebud" painted on its boards. John the Baptist is a flasher in a dirty trench coat who sprays the contents of a seltzer bottle on those who doubt his ministry. Mary Magdalene is chased by an angry crowd across a lawn in a manner reminiscent of the closing credits in Benny Hill's television show while the adult Jesus is a cigarette smoking womanizer who consults with an astrologer and gives in to His mother's demands to turn water into wine for her personal consumption.

McWilliams slices clips from old flicks into his offering, with scenes from the Babylon segment of *Intolerance* to enhance Herod's hedonism and an old-school chorus line accompanying Salome's celebrated dance. Far less endearing is a brutally unfunny joke about Holocaust gas chambers and a Last Supper scene when the Disciples drop their food on a buffet table and scatter in disgust when Jesus refers to the bread and wine as His body and blood. The Crucifixion occurs while the Disciples play Monopoly at the foot of the cross, a seedy salesman peddles souvenirs of the ongoing deicide, and a pregnant teen girl waves goodbye to the dying Jesus who left her with a new life to raise.

The Divine Mr. J wound up getting a New York City premiere in May 1974 not because of its stupid contents, but because of an unlikely cast member: Bette Midler was still an unknown talent when she was paid $250 for her 10-minute role as the Virgin Mary. The film's title was a riff on Midler's breakthrough 1972 album *The Divine Miss M*, and the caricature of Midler that appeared on her eponymous second album was used without permission in the advertising for this film, along with the incorrect insistence that this was her film debut. (She had an unbilled bit part in the 1966 epic *Hawaii*.)

Mercifully for audiences expecting to see professional quality filmmaking, *The Divine Mr. J* flopped in its brief New York City run and threats by Midler's lawyers of a lawsuit claiming false advertising kept the film from gaining any theatrical traction. The film re-emerged in 1984 on VHS video under the title *The Thorn* (obviously a joke inspired by the Midler feature *The Rose*), but more threats from Midler's lawyers resulted in the film being permanently withdrawn from commercial release.

The Phony Jesus

The 1970s also witnessed a pair of films that all but called out Jesus for being a fraud. The first came in 1971, when Dalton Trumbo adapted and directed his 1938 novel *Johnny Got His Gun*. Timothy Bottoms starred as Joe Bonham, a teenage World War I soldier who loses all of his limbs and has most of his face blown off during the conflict. Lying in a heavily bandaged state in an isolated hospital room, the soldier drifts in and out of memories and dreams – with Jesus appearing in two dream sequences.

In the first dream, Jesus is kibitzing with a group of soldiers engaged in a card game – He turns one soldier's glass of water into whiskey, happily explaining the feat by saying, "I used to do it at weddings." Joe realizes that the soldiers in the dream have all died in battle, and that Jesus is leading them off to their deaths – an effect depicted by a happy Jesus leaning out of the conductor's window of a fast-moving train and howling into the night sky.

In the second dream, Jesus forsakes his traditional white robe and is wearing a leather apron. The setting is a carpenter's shop – a stack of wooden crosses is piled in the back – and Jesus signs a deliveryman's invoice while conversing with Joe, who describes his hopeless physical state to the Nazarene.

"Since your real life is a greater nightmare than your dreams," Jesus tells Joe, "it would be cruel to pretend that anyone can help you. What you need is a miracle." Jesus adds sourly, "Perhaps it would be better for you to go away now. You're a very unlucky young man and sometimes it rubs off."

Trumbo cast Donald Sutherland as Jesus and fitted him with a flowing blonde wig – but there was little holiness to be found in his presentation. To his credit, Sutherland underplayed the role and smoothed out the abrasive characterization of Jesus as a charlatan by adding a level of charisma that is absent from the other actors in Trumbo's drearily heavy-handed film. This Jesus might have been a con artist, but at least Sutherland made him an appealing one.

A more strident denunciation of Jesus' divinity came with the 1976 drama *The Passover Plot*. The film was based on a controversial 1965 book by British Biblical scholar Hugh J. Schonfield that argued Jesus was a man who schemed to take advantage of ancient prophecies by creating a following that would recognize Him as the long-awaited Messiah, at which point He would lead a rebellion by the Jewish people against the Roman occupation force in the Holy Land.

Schonfield's theory was capped by an astonishing consideration: Jesus arranged to be arrested and crucified, and that He planned to survive the Crucifixion through the use of analgesic drugs given to Him in wine while He was on the cross. In this scam, Jesus would fake His resurrection, thus giving the false impression of the ancient prophecies being fulfilled. However, this plan was ruined when a Roman centurion pierced the side of the crucified Jesus with a spear, thus ensuring death. Schonfield concluded the story of the Resurrection was a hoax perpetrated by the Gospels authors who created their works decades after Jesus' death.

While Schonfield's notions had no problems attracting readers, the idea of a film that rewrote the Gospels in such an unusual manner did not appeal to Hollywood. Eleven years passed after the publication of *The Passover Plot* before a low-budget film produced by the low-rent Israeli team of Menahem Golan and Yoram Globus sought to dramatize Schonfield's theories.

Needless to say, *The Passover Plot* was the most curious Jesus film imaginable. As played by Zalman King, Jesus – called Yeshua of Nazareth – is a cynical zealot who orchestrates His campaign with the bland cunning of a political operative. The film also gives complete absolution to the Sanhedrin, insisting that Pontius Pilate (played by Donald Pleasance) was aware of Yeshua's activities from the start and coerced the feeble elderly Caiaphas (Hugh Griffith) to hold the trial that would seal Yeshua's faith. Even Judas – called Judah here and played by Scott Wilson of *In Cold Blood* fame – received his 30 pieces of silver directly from a Roman general and not the Sanhedrin leadership.

The Passover Plot could have been an offensive assault on Christian beliefs, but the film was too incompetent to make any serious intellectual damage. Director Michael Campus, who was best known for his B-level Blaxploitation flicks *The Mack* (1973) and *The Education of Sonny Campus* (1974), failed to inject any degree of emotional involvement into the production. Adam Greenberg's dull cinematography only reaffirmed the sense of monotony. Except for when a few of the actors were eager to overplay their roles – particularly Harry Andrews as the wild and rather woolly "Yohanan the Baptist" – or when the film inexplicably gets detoured with anachronistic solarization effects, the proceedings had a dingy, dreary, enervated personality.

The Passover Plot made almost no impact upon its release – critics were dismissive and no studio would touch it, thus forcing its producers to self-distribute the work on a limited theatrical platform. The film did earn a mild hiccup of prestige when it received a surprise Academy Award nomination for Best Costume Design – but that was more of a tribute to designer Mary Willis' standing within her profession than to the uninteresting Biblical garb she sewed together for this production.

The Three Jesus Musicals of 1973

In 1973, movie audiences had a choice of three musicals based on the life of Jesus. All of these offered an unusual consideration of Jesus' mission and ministry, albeit with varying degrees of success.

Two of the films, *Godspell* and *Jesus Christ Superstar*, seemed like different sides of the same coin. Both originated in 1971 as theatrical productions: *Godspell* as a popular off-Broadway work written by John-Michael Tebelak with music and lyrics by Stephen Schwartz, *Jesus Christ Superstar* as a West End and Broadway presentation based on a rock opera album by Andrew Lloyd Weber and Tim Rice.

The film adaptations also mirrored each other in too many ways. The theatrical concepts were recast into open air works set amid vast settings – the urban canyons of Manhattan for *Godspell*, the deserts and ancient ruins of Israel for *Jesus Christ Superstar* – with large casts of little-known actors populating the screen. The directors for both films – David Greene for *Godspell*, Norman Jewison for *Jesus Christ Superstar* – also shared a curious penchant for sequences captured via telephoto lens shots that isolated the actors in a far distance amid a vast landscape; they also took initiatives with non-traditional casting, with multicultural Disciples in *Jesus Christ Superstar* and a mix of female and male Disciples in *Godspell*.

Even more unusual was the near-identical manner in which both films considered Jesus. The films made no reference of His birth or childhood and introduced Him well into his adulthood – with the John the Baptist encounter in *Godspell* and the period before the procession into Jerusalem in *Jesus Christ Superstar*. Neither film showed Jesus performing miracles, although *Jesus Christ Superstar* alluded to His curative feats and included a scene where Jesus is overwhelmed by lepers seeking His healing power. Both films emphasized Jesus' humanity and downplayed His divinity – with the lyrics to "I Don't Know How to Love Him" from *Jesus Christ Superstar* going so far to comment on how "He's a man, He's just a man." And, more remarkably, both films ended with the Crucifixion, with no consideration of the Resurrection that followed.

In shooting *Godspell* in Manhattan, director Greene stressed the contemporary relevance of the Gospels. The most successful element of the film is the opening sequence, where working-class New Yorkers are enchanted away from their dreary jobs through the unexpected appearance of John the Baptist (played by David Haskell) and his blasting of the shofar that opens the song "Prepare Ye the Way of the Lord." The New Yorkers abandon their duties, change their clothing into funky hippie threads and leave the burdens of the city – not to mention the city's other residents, who promptly vanish from sight while the Disciples gather at Central Park's Bethesda Fountain (with its oversized angel statue in the center of the water) to be born anew.

Godspell tries to keep a positive and peppy vibe, but the camera magnifies the intense cheerfulness of the cast and the result often feels like a film that is too cute for its own good. And there are more than a few moments where the cast goes skipping along with inane merriment down Manhattan's wide avenues.

Godspell's Jesus, as played by Victor Garber, is a goofy and cheerful character sporting an oversized afro, clown make-up around his eyes, bright suspenders, oversized shoes and (in a facetiously cute touch) a Superman shirt. Garber was taller than his fellow players, but he was never framed as an otherworldly entity. Indeed, He blended in with the film's ensemble, mixing it up in the vaudeville-style skits used to bring the Parables to life and sharing the song-and-dance numbers without dominating the sequences. Garber's Jesus may be the smartest person in the room, but He's also one of the gang – a very uncommon cinematic depiction of Jesus.

Presenting the Parables with a heavy emphasis on mugging and double takes gives the impression that Jesus spoke softly and carried a big shtick. But that happy-silly approach doesn't work when the film presents Jesus facing His enemies. Rather than risk accusations of anti-Semitism, *Godspell* reimagines the Sanhedrin as an gigantic puppet monster. It is a silly notion, especially in view of the intentionally ramshackle nature of the creation, and it offers an unnecessary blurring of the fundamental issues that targeted Jesus for persecution and death.

This situation is further complicated in the film's last scenes, where Judas' betrayal seals Jesus' fate. The Last Supper is held in a former junkyard cleaned up by the Disciples and Judas – whose Biblical lines are recited by David Haskell, which creates a disturbing dichotomy considering his earlier turn as John the Baptist. He runs off for his betrayal and returns with several police cars that park outside of the junkyard fence. One might think that *Godspell* would reinvent the Roman centurions as the New York Police Department, but the cops never appear to carry out the Crucifixion. Instead, Judas conducts the murder unilaterally by tying Jesus' wrists to a fence with long red ribbons. Immobilized in the agony of the cross with His arms outstretched, Jesus suffers quickly and dies. The Disciples, in grief, take Him down from the fence and hold him over their heads with His arms still outstretched from the Crucifixion position. Chanting "Long Live God," they carry the dead Jesus through the city, turning a corner and disappearing from sight. The camera tracks after them, and suddenly the city is alive again with its population – the Disciples and Jesus are absent from view, but present on the soundtrack.

While *Godspell* uses skits and sketches to illustrate Jesus' teaching, *Jesus Christ Superstar* takes the show business scene as the foundation of its existence. That film opens with a busload of performers who arrive at an isolated spot in the Israeli desert and unload the costumes and props (including an oversized cross) from their vehicle. The performers wander about the site of an ancient temple and the story commences with a focus on Judas (played by Carl Anderson, a Black singer/actor who broke racial barriers with his casting).

Jesus Christ Superstar is unique in trying to magnify the emotional angst behind Judas' betrayal of Jesus. The reason, according to the film, was Judas' growing disillusionment with Jesus' shifting emphasis from generic acts of intellectual benevolence into creating a cult based on His perceived self-deification.

Further confusing Judas is Jesus' behavior. As interpreted through Ted Neeley's performance, Jesus is an aloof and sometimes unpleasant individual who enjoys the lavish attentions from Mary

Magdalene and becomes peeved when His action and judgment is called into question. Neeley might be the most emotionally complex Jesus in movie history, with behavior that violently swings between emotional levels.

This drama is viewed by the priests of the Sanhedrin, who are seen occupying the scaffolding around the ruins of a temple. They are threatened by and jealous of Jesus' appeal to the masses and happily manipulate the conflicted Judas into having Jesus arrested.

While *Jesus Christ Superstar* deserves credit for daring to reshape the story by trying to explain Judas' point of view and behavior, the film is frequently undercut by Tim Rice's lyrics, which traffic too heavily concentrated in flippant colloquialisms and intentional anachronisms – the most notorious being when the gleeful hedonist Herod Antipas commands Jesus to "walk across my swimming pool." Rice's lyrics are often too clever for their own good and wind up demeaning the story with crass jokes rather than enhancing it with cerebral wit.

And, quite frankly, the film is not helped by central performers who are not very good actors. Neeley's vocalizing is not particularly vibrant – the film's producers reportedly considered Mick Jagger, John Lennon, and even David Cassidy before casting Neeley. And his physical presence is underwhelming – after the arrest in the Garden of Gethsemane, Neeley is dwarfed by the studly actors playing the centurions, which gives the odd impression of Jesus being a small man amid a musclebound Roman occupation. The sequence that should be the showstopper, the intense "Gethsemane" number, is reduced to blandness by Neeley's enervated singing and mild screen presence. Even in anger, Neeley never plumbs the fury of Jesus, and instead he merely breaks loose with screeching in a higher note.

Anderson is a much better singer than Neeley, but his acting is not special and he never captures the throbbing desperation of Judas' doubts. Instead, he resorts to singing louder when frustrated by his dilemma, but in this case turning up the volume is not the same thing as turning in a performance. The same problems burdened Yvonne Elliman's Mary Magdalene, who is a musical joy and a dramatic zero. Only Joshua Mostel's Herod Antipas registers with audiences, bringing an unapologetic hedonism in his wicked display of ancient Judean vulgarity and crude mockery of the prisoner brought before him.

The only time when *Jesus Christ Superstar* truly feels like a work of imagination is the title song number, which is envisioned as a dream of Jesus between the hours of His condemnation by Pilate and the Crucifixion. Judas, who hanged himself earlier, is a ghostly figure lowered into an amphitheater via a crane and he joins a chorus of disco-clad singers and dancers to belt out the title song with an emotional gusto that was strangely absent from the earlier footage. When the film concludes with the Crucifixion with the performers returning to their bus to venture home, Anderson is the last person on the vehicle, looking out with an enigmatic expression at the cross left standing at Calvary – and, one might assume, with Jesus still nailed to it, as His burial was not shown and Neeley is not clearly visible among the performers getting on the bus.

Jesus Christ Superstar would be filmed on two more occasions for non-theatrical presentation: in a 2000 direct-to-video production and in a live 2018 telecast on NBC. (A film was released in the Philippines in 1972 with the same title, but the story and music were different from the Weber-Rice production.) To date, there have been no additional film versions of *Godspell*, although the show continues to be staged theatrically in both its original version and in a *Godspell Jr.* offering that edits the original for presentation by student theater groups.

The third Jesus musical of 1973 was the most idiosyncratic of the trio. *Gospel Road: A Story of Jesus* was created by the country music icon Johnny Cash, who credited his Christian faith in helping him to overcome professional and personal obstacles. When asked why he was making the film, Cash said, "I think Jesus was the most misquoted, misread and misunderstood man in history. People have twisted His words to suit their needs. People also died for Him. They died for His words."

Cash self-financed the production – the budget has been cited as being between $500,000 and $1 million, although there is a good chance it was actually lower. *Gospel Road*, like *Jesus Christ Superstar*, was shot on location in Israel. But unlike the other two musical films of the era, the musical numbers were performed on the soundtrack while Jesus and those of His world are depicted by non-professional actors in dialogue-free sequences. (The players in the film were a mix of Cash's family and friends along with tourists in Israel who were visiting the locations where the film was being shot and wound up being corralled before the camera.)

The film is almost entirely narrated by Cash, who occasionally appears on screen in his trademark black clothing while clutching an open Bible. Cash describes the life and ministry of Jesus in a mix of readings from the New Testament, personal observations, and a wealth of original music that is played on the soundtrack.

The idea of having a wall-to-wall narration against a panto-mimed presentation might seem dull, but Cash was a narrator of undeniable charisma and his force of personality makes *Gospel Road* an invigorating and deeply personal experience. He approached the film with a sense of sincerity rather than an air of academia, and the result was a genuine emotional bond with the subject that is missing from most Biblical films. And, of course, that Johnny Cash voice was always invigorating, whether he was speaking or singing.

Most of the musical soundtrack consists of gospel-tinged works sung by Cash, with some selections performed by the Statler Brothers, Larry Gatlin, the Carter Family, Kris Kristofferson and Rita Coolidge, and Cash's wife June Carter Cash, who was cast as Mary Magdalene and performed the film's best-known song, the John Denver-penned "Follow Me." Whereas many critics look back at *Godspell* and *Jesus Christ Superstar* and bemoan that their respective scores are anchored in a specific era, the music of *Gospel Road* has a timeless element. A few songs had appeared publicly prior to the film's production: "He Turned the Water into Wine" and "Jesus Was a Carpenter" were from earlier Cash albums, while Larry Gatlin's "Help Me" and Denver's "Follow Me" were performed in cover versions for the film.

Cash initially conceived Jesus as an elusive entity who would only be seen by His feet. However, Cash realized that approach would not work. The star and his wife considered several casting choices before deciding on the *Gospel Road* director, Swedish-born filmmaker Robert Elfstrom, to play Jesus. With his blonde hair, blue eyes and fair skin, Elfstrom was not your typical Nazarene. Elfstrom's son, Robert Jr., who shared his father's Scandinavian appearance, appeared briefly as a pre-teen Jesus – as with the other musicals, there is no recreation of the Nativity or of Jesus' miraculous healings. (Elfstrom came to this film after previously directing the 1969 documentary *Johnny Cash! The Man, His World, His Music.*)

But while Elfstrom may not have been physically correct for the role, his performance was remarkable for capturing the softer side of Jesus' humanity. In this film, Jesus is seen at ease with all around Him, even laughing with His Disciples and enjoying the company of playful children. This easy-going Jesus is capable of solemnity and, when applicable, anger, and the multiple phases of behavior frame Jesus with a dimensionality that is missing in too many films that imagine Him solely as a being in a fixed, single emotional state.

As a director, Elfstrom brings in a number of remarkable artistic moments. During Jesus' baptism by John the Baptist, Jesus' perspective is shown in a stunning POV shot from beneath the water looking up at John. When emerging from the baptism, a white dove unexpectedly lands on Jesus' shoulder, offering a surprise symbolic appearance by the Holy Spirit. The film recreates the story of the woman accused of adultery, but it does not conflate that woman with Mary Magdalene, who is seen here as a salt-of-the-earth type of woman.

Furthermore, Elfstrom telescopes the prosecution of Jesus by presenting His three hostile judges – Caiaphas, Pilate and Herod Antipas – together, each framed with an arc of ancient ruin. Jesus' crucifixion takes place on a cross that is considerably shorter than those used in other Biblical films, which gives the disturbing impression of a torturous death occurring at eye level. But what is truly striking is what transpires during Jesus' death: the cross bearing the dying Jesus is unexpectedly shown against several modern urban landscapes, where traffic whizzes by in seeming modern indifference to the sacrifice made on the cross centuries earlier.

Gospel Road is a fascinating endeavor with a distinctive personality. In an interview with Cash biographer Robert Hillburn, Elfstrom credited Cash as being an indefatigable spirit in bringing the film to life.

"John put his heart into this film," Elfstrom said, recalling the pre-production period in Israel. "He was up with me at 3:30 in the morning, going out to various sites, and then he'd come to my room in his pajamas at night, and we'd figure out the scene for the next day."

20th Century-Fox picked up the theatrical distribution rights from Cash and initially released the film primarily in the South, with Northeast playdates sparingly scheduled months after the film ran its course in Southern theaters. The double-album soundtrack album was one of the most popular music releases of 1973. Cash gave permission to Billy Graham to screen the film at his religious crusades, and the film found new audiences in 2005 with a DVD release that was timed to the distribution of the Cash biopic *I Walk the Line*.

The Elusive Jesus

During the mid-1970s, a pair of independently produced feature films with decidedly unique perspectives on the life of Jesus snaked their way through brief theatrical releases before vanishing from sight. Neither *The Rebel Jesus* nor *Him* have been seen since playing in theaters, and their prolonged absence has raised a high degree of curiosity and speculation regarding their oddball contents.

The Rebel Jesus was an unusual entry in the canon of Larry Buchanan, a Dallas-based filmmaker who gained a degree of cinematic infamy for his output of micro-budget exploitation and science-fiction features, including *Mars Needs Women*, *Curse of the Swamp Creature* and *Zontar, the Thing from Venus*. Buchanan claimed that he wrote the script for *The Rebel Jesus* 10 years prior to its 1972 production – but in view of Buchanan's penchant for piggybacking his quickie films to cash in on current events (most notably with the 1964 docudrama *The Trial of Lee Harvey Oswald*) and major Hollywood works (the 1968 effort *The Other Side of Bonnie and Clyde*), it would not be snide to wonder if Buchanan chose religion-on-film to cash in on the twin productions of *Jesus Christ Superstar* and *Godspell* that were being prepared.

In typical Buchanan fashion, *The Rebel Jesus* seeks an off-kilter storyline. In this case, Jesus does not die on the cross, but survives the Crucifixion and is rescued by a secretive religious sect and is taken to a brothel where Mary Magdalene nurses Him back to health. However, a Roman centurion who was assigned to the Crucifixion learns of Jesus' escape from His death sentence and vows to carry out the Pilate-decreed execution.

The notion of Jesus cheating death on the cross bears more than a passing resemblance to Hugh J. Schonfield's 1965 book *The Passover Plot* and its aforementioned film adaptation. Buchanan never cited Schonfield's book in his 1997 autobiography *It Came from Hunger: Tales of a Cinema Schlockmeister*, but he focused on the numerous difficulties he encountered in shooting his $170,000 feature in Tunisia – as with Pasolini, he claimed that he could not shoot in Israel because the country had become so modernized that he was unable to find appropriate locations to double for Biblical settings. Buchanan never explained why he cast Gene Shane, a B-movie actor best known for flicks like *Werewolves on Wheels* and *Blood of Dracula's Castle*, in the title role or why Erica Gavin, the bosomy starlet of *Beyond the Valley of the Dolls* fame, accepted and then dropped out of the Mary Magdalene role.

One unlikely collaborator that Buchanan brought to this project was Alex North, the acclaimed Hollywood composer. Buchanan said that he was acquainted with North since they were both new to the film world in the 1950s and the Oscar-nominated composer was happy to work within Buchanan's highly restrictive budget to create and record a memorable music score.

While Buchanan's work as a director may have left a lot to be desired, his ability to generate publicity about himself was peerless. Indeed, some of the comments that Buchanan made about *The Rebel Jesus* for the press are entertaining for their sheer outrageousness. In an October 1972 interview with syndicated columnist James Bacon, Buchanan insisted that American International Pictures wanted him to make *The Rebel Jesus* as "a bike picture, a modern allegory." He also stated that Universal Pictures expressed interest in obtaining distribution rights to *The Rebel Jesus* in order to keep it out of release while that studio's big-budget presentation of *Jesus Christ Superstar* took over the theaters.

In a November 1972 interview with the Associated Press, Buchanan became even edgier in hyping his film as an assault on the conventional concept of the Gospels.

"It's not a church-basement movie," he said. "But it's not anti-Christ, either. It's more of the Christ of Albert Schweitzer, Father Cavanaugh and Bishop Pike, against the Christ of Billy Graham."

Buchanan also trash talked the two Jesus-focused musicals that *The Rebel Jesus* was going up against. "*Jesus Christ Superstar* is a rip-off; there's nothing new there," he continued. "The authors failed to introduce anything to help us understand the man. *Godspell* is a better approach, but it still fails to offer anything that is new."

If that wasn't enough, Buchanan upped the ante in stirring controversy with an August 1973 interview published by the syndicated Newspaper Enterprise Association.

"Inevitably, there will be organized opposition to our film," he proclaimed. "Hard-shelled fundamentalists will be offended, because we differ from what is in the Bible. It's all our own story, although lots of people have postulated the thesis that Jesus survived the cross. Any time you're dealing with de-mythology, you're in trouble, and that's what we're doing."

Despite his assurances to the media that *The Rebel Jesus* would be in theaters before *Jesus Christ Superstar* and *Godspell*, Buchanan's film did not get its initial presentation until the 1973 Atlanta Film Festival, where it won a Bronze Medal in the "Low Budget Feature" category. Theatrical playdates were booked in four-walled engagements in the Texas cities of Amarillo and Commerce, but then Buchanan abruptly pulled *The Rebel Jesus* from release. He later stated that he felt his work was incomplete and he vowed not to re-release it until he felt he got it right.

Buchanan died in 2004, having completed and released six additional films before returning to and reportedly completing this work. Buchanan gave *The Rebel Jesus* the new name of *The Copper Scroll of Mary Magdalene*, which suggests inspiration from the New Testament apocrypha *The Gospel of Mary* – although the narrative of that ancient text bears no resemblance to Buchanan's Jesus-in-a-brothel plot.

But what changes did Buchanan bring to his film? It is impossible to determine – to date, the film has never been made available for screening. Buchanan's advocacy of quality control on this production is especially peculiar, considering that he put forth a body of low-grade work that The *New York Times* described as "deeply, dazzlingly, unrepentantly bad."

Was the normally shameless Buchanan embarrassed by this particular film? Or did he feel that his revisionist approach to the life of Jesus pushed the proverbial envelope much too far? The latter is a possible theory – in his autobiography, Buchanan shared a vitriolic letter he sent to Martin Scorsese that excoriated the master director for *The Last Temptation of Christ*. It is not known if Scorsese responded to the letter, or if he even saw it.

Even more mysterious is the 1974 film *Him* (sometimes spelled as *HIM*). Most moviegoers never heard of it until Harry and Michael Medved's 1979 book *The Golden Turkey Awards*, which celebrated what they considered to be the most outrageous bad movies of all time. *Him* was a gay porn film that the Medveds cited as the prime example of the "Most Unerotic Concept in Pornography." Indeed, the Medveds did not lavish their snarky humor on describing Him, turning instead to a level of self-righteous indignation over the film's contents.

"For sheer tastelessness, this film has no equals," the Medveds wrote. "Those pathetic few who might want to see *Him* ought to come to the theater dressed in plain, brown paper wrappers, that hopefully cover their eyes along with the rest of their faces."

Whether the Medveds went to a gay porn theater to see the film is not clear – openly-gay columnist Andrew Sullivan challenged Michael Medved for an answer, which Medved never provided. From the description of the film in *The Golden Turkey Awards*, it is possible that the Medveds may have learned of the film from a brief mainstream newspaper review of the production. (Yes, back in the day major media reviewed X-rated films playing in porn cinemas.)

Over the years, no trace of *Him* could be found beyond the Medveds' book; complicating matters was the Medveds' mention of someone named Ed D. Louie as the director of this work – his name was nowhere to be celebrated in any resource relating to adult cinema. The mystery surrounding this filmmaker led some Internet buzz generators to speculate that Mr. Louie was none other than the celebrated schlockmeister Edward D. Wood Jr., who had ended his career making X-rated films under pseudonyms.

The *Pimpadelic Wonderland* website tried to find *Him* in the early 2000s but had no luck locating a print, and in 2003 it listed the film as lost. In 2008, the author of this book included the film in a *Film Threat* article on the 50 most intriguing lost films of all time. Incredibly, the inclusion of *Him* on that list set off a firestorm among several professional archivists who were members of the Association of Moving Image Archivists' list-serv – those scholars claimed that *Him* never existed, and their evidence was the claim by the Medveds that they intentionally planted a hoax film in *The Golden Turkey Awards*. The anger of the archivists was the subject of an article on *Fishbowl NY*, a now-defunct online site covering the New York-area media industry.

But the professional know-it-alls were wrong about *Him* being a hoax. The hoax film in *The Golden Turkey Awards* was something called *Dog of Norway*. Perhaps the idea of a gay porn film about Jesus was too upsetting for some people to accept, hence the archivists' fury.

So, what was the story of *Him*? What was it really all about? And what became of the film?

One person deserves credit for trying to piece together much of the mystery: a blogger who goes by the name Captain Obscurity. Writing on a website called *To Obscurity and Beyond*, this intrepid cinematic detective has been able to dig up a surprising amount of detail about this elusive title.

"In this age of DVD imports and online streaming it sometimes feels like film is immortal, like we have access to everything ever made and always will," said Captain Obscurity. "Lost films remind us that that is not the case, which is sad, but there is an exciting side to it too; the mystery and intrigue aren't dead. Anyway, of all the films mentioned on *Pimpadelic Wonderland*, *Him* probably had the least info: just a newspaper ad and a note saying it was a gay porn take on the life of Christ. Initially I was no more interested in *Him* than any of the other films, it was only after I found people on web forums and blogs claiming that it had never existed, that the whole thing was a hoax, that I really got into researching it further. At the time, Google had just launched its searchable scanned newspaper archive, and with some creative Google-fu I was able to track down more ads and even a few reviews."

Captain Obscurity's initial findings confirmed that *Him* played in New York at the 55th Street Playhouse, a venue specializing in gay porn titles, back in the spring of 1974. To his delight, he found that he was not alone in searching out this mysterious work.

"Another guy I met on a web forum – he calls himself Billy A. Anderson online, I don't think that's his real name – did a lot of work too, digging out Al Goldstein's write-up from an old edition of *Screw* and also tracking down info on performances outside the 55th Street Playhouse," he continued. "At first, the research was purely to satisfy my own curiosity, but given the amount of info we turned up - whilst the uninformed were still calling it vapor - I decided it would be smart to put all the evidence together in one place where people would see it."

Al Goldstein's review gives far more detail regarding the film's plot – and it appears to contradict the Medveds' claim that Jesus was the central character of the film. Goldstein noted that "the movie begins inexorably slowly and, for its first 40 minutes, it consists of some solid hard-core in the gay vein and the meaning of the title *Him* eludes the spectator. Only deeply into the film does one get the necessary material to permit the audience to comprehend the meaning of the plot."

Goldstein viewed the film with mixed emotions, claiming it was "bizarrely engrossing" yet complaining that it was littered with "mismatched shots, mishmash editing and [a] cheap budget." But Goldstein gave no hint that the film's detour into religion would spark outrage if those beyond its core audience would discover it – and Captain Obscurity offers a reminder that films like *Him* were not unusual for their time.

"There's an interesting sociological aspect in there: if something like *Him* played in theaters today, there would be an uproar," he explained. "In 1974, no one batted an eyelid. The funny thing is, it's not even the only hardcore Jesus movie made around that time. You probably already know about the European adult movie *I Saw Jesus Die*, but when I was researching *Him*, I stumbled upon another gay picture called *Loadstar* which also, supposedly, features Jesus engaging in sexual acts with men. That one came out just a year or so before *Him* was shot in Los Angeles and also featured a scene with ostensibly straight bodybuilder (and associate of Arnold Schwarzenegger) Bob Birdsong. All these dirty Christ movies were doing the rounds in the 1970s and there's little evidence of protests or threats or anything like that. Five years later, *Life of Brian* came out and almost sparked a holy war. What a strange decade!"

Mercifully, there were enough survivors of that strange decade who found their way to the Internet to confirm seeing *Him* when it was in theaters. And this includes a pair of individuals who had connections to the people involved in this film.

First up is Wakefield Poole, the pioneering adult filmmaker who scored the first major commercial gay porn success with the 1971 *Boys in the Sand*. In an email interview, Poole clearly remembered the mysterious Ed D. Louie (real name: Ed Lui) and he confirmed that he was not the celebrated Edward D. Wood Jr.

"The most I can tell you is that Ed Lui was the manager of the 55th St. Theater at the time I four-walled it to open *Boys in The Sand*," Poole recalled, referring to the practice of a filmmaker proactively renting a cinema for a theatrical exhibition. "He was a relative of Frank Lee, who had the lease on the theater for years. With the success of my films, it turned out to be a gold mine for him. Of course, he never put any money back into the theater. A few years later, Mr. Louie, as we called him, decided to make a film and cash in. Unfortunately, he was a little late. The theater was run down, with no air conditioner, and loaded with pickpockets. There was no audience left."

Poole also saw *Him*, and he did not find the experience overwhelming.

"I saw the film the first day," he continued. "I only remember it was painful to watch. It was underexposed, badly edited, obviously made to cause a fuss and make lots of money. Unfortunately, I don't remember any moments from the film. I must have been very drugged. I think it only ran for a few days. It didn't make money, but still remains a great mystery in the history of porn."

Actually, Poole is off concerning one detail: the 55th Street Playhouse run of *Him* ran from March 27 to May 23 in 1974.

In July 2012, Captain Obscurity snagged another big breakthrough: a New York artist named Vinny Parrillo saw his online research on *Him* and identified the actor who played Jesus as his late partner, a muralist named Gustav Von Will who acted in the film under the stage name Tava. Parrillo also produced a photo of Tava in character as a naked Jesus carrying a cross through Manhattan, which presented the first (and, to date, only) production still from *Him* to emerge.

According to film scholar Jack Holman, it is possible that scenes from the film were edited into a reel now in the collection of Kinsey Institute Library at Indiana University. This reel features scenes from a number of gay porn productions released by distribution company Hand in Hand Films. At the moment, the extant *Him* remains missing. It seems unlikely that more than one or two release prints of *Him* were struck back in 1974, as there is no confirmed evidence that the film played in more than one city at a time. But even if it did turn up today, Captain Obscurity would not be eager to view what he has been searching out for years.

"Personally, even if *Him* was found tomorrow and turned out to be some gay porn masterpiece, I'm not sure I would go out and buy a copy," he stated. "I'd be glad the mystery was solved, but if someone sent it to me, I'd probably fast forward through the screwing; I've never been a big hardcore fan, I don't consider sex a particularly interesting spectator sport; plus, I'm straight, so it's not even my favored brand of sex. It's the search I enjoy more than anything – the film is just a McGuffin."

The Indian Jesus

India's film industry never placed great emphasis on Christian-themed films, which is understandable since less than 2.5% of the country's population identify as Christian and the perceived commercial value of such productions are considered minimal. During the 1970s, a pair of feature films were produced that offered retellings of Jesus' life through the distinctive spectrum of India's cinematic styles.

The 1973 *Jesus* was produced in the Malayalam language and later dubbed into the Tamil and Telugu languages. The 1978 *Karunamayudu* was shot in Telugu and dubbed into four other Indian languages, most notably a Hindi version that received the widest release under the title *Daya Sagar*. Neither film was theatrically released in the West and both are still mostly unknown to non-Indian audiences. This is something of a shame, as they represent very different filmgoing experiences: *Jesus* offers a wealth of unintentional humor due to its spectacularly poor production, while *Daya Sagar* provides an intelligent and creative consideration of the subject despite occasional hiccups in the presentation.

Jesus starts off on the proverbial wrong foot with a seemingly indifferent Mary receiving news via an animated light shaft and a puff of yellow smoke about the baby she will soon carry. Joseph is also alerted in the same manner. While the couple travels to Bethlehem, a trio of comic relief shepherds – one plays the lyre and hums aloud while the others snore in cartoonish noises – are visited by angels that look like young girls wearing cumbersome wigs and overly upholstered gowns. Mary, Joseph, the shepherds, the Three Kings and the angels gather in an open-air manger that seems made of cardboard while the soundtrack swells to a wobbly "O Come All Ye Faithful" that turns into a Malayalam music sequence with almost everyone singing (including a cartoon Star of Bethlehem).

Old King Herod orders the Slaughter of the Innocents, but then amuses himself with some shapely belly dancers – obviously, the Gospels needed a bit of Minsky's burlesque to oomph things up. The 12-year-old Jesus abruptly appears in the temple – the kid is wearing a red wig which rivals the fake beard and grey wig that Joseph is wearing. The adult Jesus (played by the actor Murali Das) has a more robust red wig and an equally bogus red beard and walks through the film with a slight air of detachment from his surroundings, pausing only to allow animated bolts to flow from his hand for the miracles at Cana and Lazarus' tomb.

The main problem with *Jesus* is that director P.A. Thomas brings more sincerity than artistry to the screen. Much of the acting is children's theater-level broad, with extravagant gestures and over-sized emoting that leaves absolutely nothing to the imagination. Satan shows up to tempt Jesus wearing a Halloween devil costume, complete with cape, and Salome gets John the Baptist's wooly head on silver platter thanks to a great deal of sensual wiggling that probably would have gotten her stoned back in ancient Judea. Not to be outdone, Mary Magdalene has her own song-and-dance number before seeing the value in Jesus' teaching.

In fairness, *Jesus* depicts two stories that are often absent from films in this genre: the casting of Legion from the afflicted man and the Transfiguration. Alas, the former is quickly done without Legion being exiled into the swine herd while the Transfiguration is crudely staged on a cheapjack set with Moses and Elijah looking like a pair of skinny Santa Clauses.

But *Jesus* saves the best for last with the Resurrection. Rather than simply roll back the stone used as the tomb's door, Jesus bursts through the roof of the tomb in a cloud of yellow smoke and fast-forwards directly into the Ascension, with nary a TTFN to the Disciples.

Daya Sagar has some of the problems that burden *Jesus*, including lamentable animation and actors in patently false beards. But director A. Bhimsingh steers the film in unexpected ways, creating a unique interpretation of the oft-told story.

Daya Sagar starts with the Nativity as an extended music sequence, with Mary hearing a lyrical Annunciation while reading a scroll in a garden. She is visited by a blonde white-robed male angel, who then appears to the dreaming Joseph. The number is extended to the journey to Bethlehem, where a montage of doors closed to Mary and Joseph reinforces the severity of their outcast status. Oddly, Mary appears to have given birth on a grassy field, although they are quickly shown after in the manger.

After rapid glimpses of the 12-year-old Jesus at the temple and in Joseph's carpentry shop, the adult story of Jesus begins with a focus on two figures that will play key roles later in His ministry – Barabbas is shown leading rebels against Rome while the blind Bartimaeus provides a musical commentary on the society that Jesus will change. Jesus and Barabbas meet in a brief sequence later in the film, which is a curious touch – this is the only film where the two met at the point of conversation.

Perhaps the most remarkable sequence in *Daya Sagar* is the procession into Jerusalem, with masses of extras waving palms in a dance ahead of a magnificent parade to the holy city. The smile on the face of Vijayachander's Jesus is a heartwarming expression of love – prior to this, the actor played the role in a controlled and paternal manner that essayed Jesus' moral authority but missed His emotional personality. Later in the film with the torturous road to Golgotha, Vijayachander's astonishing physical performance brilliantly captured the life-draining agony of Jesus dragging the unwieldy cross to a long and painful execution – and the pause of silent relief when Veronica wipes the blood and sweat from His face is a masterful moment that captures Jesus' human existence.

Within the realm of Jesus-centric cinema, *Daya Sagar* is one of the most influential, albeit not in the West – the film has played to more than 19 million people in thousands of villages across the world, often in makeshift outdoor theaters set up with sheets connected between poles as the big screen. A missionary organization called Dayspring International has been responsible for these exhibitions, and it has claimed to have converted seven million Indians to Christianity.

Tava as Jesus in a production still from the lost 1974 pornographic feature
Him.

Chapter Five: Jesus, the Sacred and the Profane

"And everyone who speaks a word against the Son of Man will be
forgiven, but the one who blasphemes against the Holy Spirit will not
be forgiven.
– Luke 12:10

As the 1970s came to a close, the cinema seemed to divide into
two different approaches to Jesus-centric film: works of solemnity
designed to comfort the faithful and provocative works intended to
spark controversy. Let's start with the solemn.

The 1979 *Jesus* was an endeavor spearheaded by John Heyman,
who was born in Germany to Jewish parents in 1933 – Heyman's
family left Germany in the year of his birth and settled in England. Heyman went through careers as a talent agent and producer,
scoring commercial successes with projects ranging from the 1964
Broadway production of *Hamlet* starring Richard Burton to the
award-winning films *The Go-Between* and *The Hireling*.

In 1973, Heyman created the Genesis Project with the goal of
adapting all of the books of the Old and New Testament into cinematic adaptations. His initial foray involved *The New Media Bible*,
which offered 15-minute films based on the 22 chapters of Genesis
and the first two chapters of the Book of Luke. This production was
distributed to the nontheatrical educational market.

In 1976, Heyman teamed with the U.S. evangelical movement
Campus Crusade for Christ to create a feature-length film based
on Jesus' life. Heyman and Paul Eshleman, a vice president in Campus Crusade for Christ, pitched the idea of a Jesus film to the Hollywood studios, but found no takers. They secured independent
financing, including a $3 million investment from oil tycoon Bun-
ker Hunt, and ultimately raised $6 million.

Heyman and Eshelman opted to craft their film based on a
single Gospel, rather than follow the tradition of conflating the
four Gospels into a single work. They decided to shoot their film
on location in Israel, using Sephardic Jewish actors for most of the

Brian Deacon as Jesus in the 1979 production Jesus.

cast because, according to Eshelman, "their facial features have changed least over the past 2,000 years." Brian Deacon, a British actor who was primarily known for his theatrical work, was chosen to play Jesus after Heyman and Eshleman auditioned more than 260 actors for the role. Two directors, Australian Peter Sykes and Briton John Krish, were tasked to helm the project.

The resulting *Jesus* is a respectable retelling of Luke's Gospel. The film does an effective job on recreating the world of ancient Judea – the pursuit of production perfection was so strong that footage with eucalyptus trees in the scenery had to be reshot after the filmmakers realized those trees were not introduced to the region until many years after Jesus' ministry.

But while the film looks right, it is strangely lacking in personality. Much of the problem involves the Israeli cast – the filmmakers were unhappy with their handling of the English-language dialogue and had British actors dub all of their lines. But the voices never quite match the actors – although, in fairness, most of the supporting cast is given relatively little to do but look on in mild wonder at Jesus.

Brian Deacon did not require to have his lines dubbed by another actor, but it might have given some life to his line readings. Deacon's Jesus is a strangely anodyne figure who fails to generate the magnetism needed to spark a religious revolution. He mostly maintains the same low-keyed voice level and emotion-free gaze through most of the film, and this makes him one of the most lethargic Jesuses in film history.

Although Warner Bros. picked up the theatrical rights of *Jesus* for the U.S. market, the studio believed this film was not going to create a box office bonanza. *Jesus* opened in October 1979 in 250 cities in southern and western markets – it never played theatrically in the New York City market and, thus, was mostly under the radar of the major entertainment media. In fairness, Warner Bros. made an effort to promote the film to church groups, but the film never generated any degree of excitement and ended its theatrical run with a $2 million loss.

However, *Jesus* had an extraordinary second act that rescued the film from obscurity and box office ignominy. In 1980, Campus

Crusade for Christ began to dub the film into a multitude of languages for a mix of theatrical, nontheatrical, and television distribution around the world. Under Eshelman's guidance, the film was taken to India, where a Hindi-language telecast reached 21 million viewers, and to the Philippines for a Tagalog-language theatrical presentation. Within the first year of this effort, *Jesus* was translated into 31 languages – as of this writing, *Jesus* is recognized by The Guinness Book of World Records as the "Most Translated Film" in history, with translations into 1,803 languages. The Jesus Film Project, the Campus Crusade for Christ subsidiary responsible for the international distribution, claims that more than three billion people have seen *Jesus* since 1980.

In 2001, *Jesus* was the center of international news when Dayna Curry and Heather Mercer, U.S. aid workers in Afghanistan, were arrested by the Taliban for showing the film in a private screening. President George W. Bush directed the U.S. Marines to rescue the aid workers, and he greeted the liberated Americans in a White House ceremony by declaring, "It's been an uplifting experience to talk to these courageous souls."

Eshelman expressed satisfaction at the results of this work, telling the BBC in a 2004 interview that this effort gave people around the world "a chance to hear the message of Christ in an understandable language near where they live."

While this global release might seem like a mighty accomplishment, Heyman was unhappy with Campus Crusade for Christ's decision to edit the film for distribution into the many global markets where it was presented, including a version where new footage was inserted. Heyman sued his one-time partners and the case was settled out of court. Heyman would continue with his film career until his death in 2017; *Jesus* is still being dubbed into additional languages for further release to previously untapped audiences.

Also, in 1979 was a weird and wooly spin on the sacred story from a Utah-based company that went by several names including Sun International Pictures, Schick Sunn Classic Pictures and Sunn Classic Pictures. This company tapped into the growing public interest in the paranormal and historical revisionism by offering films that sought to generate controversy by challenging scientific and scholarly traditions.

The Sunn Classic titles included *Chariots of the Gods* (a 1974 English-dubbed version of an Oscar-nominated 1970 German film about alleged visits by aliens to ancient civilizations), *The Outer Space Connection* (1975), *The Mysterious Monsters* (1976), *In Search of Noah's Ark* (1976), *The Lincoln Conspiracy* (1977) and *The Bermuda Triangle* (1979). These works were paraded through distribution in a four-walling strategy where Sunn Classic rented cinemas for a limited run and saturated the local market with excessive advertising on their presentations. And while the company occasionally offered benign narrative films for the family market, most notably the 1974 *The Adventures of Grizzly Adams*, it earned its reputation for pushing the concept of nonfiction filmmaking to the most outrageous extremes.

There was one problem with the Sunn Classic canon: despite their eagerness to upend long-held beliefs and traditions with speculation on ancient aliens, contemporary aliens, and cryptozoology superstars like Bigfoot and the Loch Ness Monster, the films were always disappointing. For all of the oohs and ahhs promised in their marketing, Sunn Classic films were strictly adequate in style and often shoddy in substance. Even the best of the bunch, *Chariots of the Gods*, was fairly hesitant in fully pushing forward its thesis that the ancient Egyptians and Mayans got some help from E.T. and his pals.

By 1979, Sunn Classic seemed to be running out of ideas, so it decided to go for the ultimate shock value: a documentary questioning the mysteries of Jesus Christ while trying to figure out what events occurred during His young adult years that are not mentioned in the Gospels. Unfortunately, *In Search of Historic Jesus* was an indolent work that showed only occasional proof that its creators were vaguely familiar with its sacred subject.

Actually, the center of attention here is not Jesus, but Brad Crandall, a disk jockey who served as on-screen narrator for the production. Crandall held the same role in several Sunn Classic films, and his authoritative voice and professorial demeanor – complete with oversized dark-rimmed eyeglasses and a 1970s version of an intellectual's beard – gave the impression that he was a very smart man whose words demanded respect. Crandall's scenes were mostly shot in what looked like a library stuffed with books, as if being in the presence of books would give him an academic cred. But Crandall was not an alchemist, and his deep voice and knowledgeable demeanor could not spin cinematic gold from this leaden offering.

In Search of Historic Jesus begins its story in the Old Testament, with clips from cheapjack European epics retelling the stories of Noah, the Tower of Babel, and Joshua. The life of Jesus is presented in a scattershot manner – sort of a Greatest Hits version of the Gospels with no depth to His teachings and no understanding of the historical context of His ministry. Extras clad in unconvincing wigs and crummy costumes that would not pass the grade in a Sunday School pageant tramp around Utah locations, and a few well-known character actors including Nehemiah Persoff, Royal Dano and David Opatashu turn up in small roles.

Jesus is played by John Rubinstein, who originated the title role in the 1972 Broadway musical *Pippin* and was a familiar face in television programs during the 1970s. Rubinstein never established himself as a film star and *In Search of Historic Jesus* offers evidence on why he fell short: his line readings were bland, his charisma was nil, and he completely failed to find a sense of purpose in his character's struggles. Crandall's narration gives Rubinstein's Jesus a level of power that Rubinstein never generates. And having the actor buried under mounds of fake hair only added to the strangeness – Rubinstein seemed like a drearily polite Neanderthal rather than the Messiah.

What little fun exists in *In Search of Historic Jesus* can be found when the film strays from the Gospel to create a new history for Jesus. In one scene, Jesus tames a wild tiger – the big cat's presence in the Holy Land is never explained. Elsewhere, we have theories on what Jesus was up to during the so-called missing years. One idea finds him in Persia, another finds him in Tibet, and a third has Joseph of Arimathea taking the teenage Jesus to England on a tin-purchasing trip. The film also places Joseph back in England after Jesus' resurrection, and posits that He was buried in Glastonbury. *In Search of Historic Jesus* also mines the Mormon theology to place the resurrected Jesus in North America to confer with several tribes before making His final ascent to Heaven.

A good deal of *In Search of Historic Jesus* considers the Shroud of Turin and whether it offers the image of the crucified Jesus in its threads. And while the film would like to use this issue to affirm Jesus' holiness, it makes an intellectually unsatisfactory argument about the shroud's value as evidence of Jesus' existence.

Nonetheless, audiences overlooked the film's many flaws. Not unlike the other Sunn Classic films, *In Search of Historic Jesus* was a box office hit, raking in $22.4 million to become the 34th highest grossing film of 1979.

The third Jesus-centric film from 1979 made the greatest impact on popular culture for its sheer audacity and the brief controversy that surrounded its release. *Monty Python's Life of Brian* was created by the six-man British Monty Python comedy group – Graham Chapman, John Cleese, Eric Idle, Terry Gilliam, Terry Jones and Michael Palin – who had achieved international popularity through their television series *Monty Python's Flying Circus* (1969-1974) and two feature films, *And Now for Something Completely Different* (1971) and *Monty Python and the Holy Grail* (1975).

During the promotion of *Monty Python and the Holy Grail*, Eric Idle joked during an interview that the group's next project would be called *Jesus Christ: Lust for Glory*. As Idle and his teammates would later recall, they began to conduct research into Jesus' life but found almost nothing that they could use for a comedy film.

"It was quite obvious that there was very little to ridicule in Jesus's life, and therefore we were onto a loser," said Michael Palin in a 1979 interview. "Jesus was a very straight, direct man making good sense, so we decided it would be a very shallow film if it was just about him."

The focus was then shifted to a new character inserted by the Pythons into the Gospels: Brian Cohen, a 13th disciple whose presence was never recorded because of his chronic lateness in arriving at the key moments in Jesus' ministry. But this concept also failed to click, so it was agreed that Brian would be reconfigured as a hapless bumbler who happened to live in Judea at the time of Jesus but was mistaken for a Messiah by fanatical masses eager to find someone to liberate them against the Roman occupation.

When *Monty Python's Life of Brian* was filmed, Jesus only turned up in two fleeting scenes: as an infant in the Nativity when the Three Kings mistakenly arrive at the birth of Brian (with Terry Jones in marvelously awful drag as Brian's mother) and then have to retrieve their gifts of gold, frankincense and myrrh to be presented in the manger while Mary and Joseph watch, and later as a distant figure giving the Sermon on the Mount. In the latter scene, Jesus is so distant from those standing at the far fringes of the event that people mistakenly believe He is giving the benediction "Blessed are the cheese makers."

Instead of having fun with Jesus, *Monty Python's Life of Brian* aims its comic wrath at the social extremes of Roman-occupied Judea. The local population has a surplus of political militants who use the vaguest suggestion of religious zealotry to excuse their violently anti-social behavior, while the Roman aristocracy are presented as clueless and dimwitted hedonists who uphold their reign with casual cruelty.

The Pythons had the commitment from EMI Films to finance the production, but chief executive Bernard Delfont only read the finished screenplay prior to the start of shooting and abruptly withdrew funding out of fear that the finished work would be subject to condemnations of blasphemy. It briefly seemed that the project would have been terminated, but an unlikely rescue came from George Harrison, the former Beatle who was looking to get into film production. Harrison teamed with his American attorney and business partner Denis O'Brien to form Handmade Films, and he mortgaged his home to quickly round up the £2 million ($4.1 million) needed to fund the production. Harrison was given a bit part in the film and Eric Idle jested that his financial largesse was "the most expensive cinema ticket" ever issued.

Monty Python's Life of Brian was fairly typical of the Python style, mixing sophisticated banter with happily sophomoric sight gags. Many critics would lament that the film had a hit-and-miss element to its story. But if the film shines in bits and pieces rather than as a cohesive whole, those bits and pieces are priceless: a stoning of a blasphemer where the crowd readying the death sentence are all women struggling to maintain their bearded disguises as men, Brian's mother angrily informing the masses "He's not the Messiah, he's a very naughty boy," the Roman consul with an impossible speech impediment and a scatological name, and the extraordinary conclusion where Brian and others condemned to die in crucifixions meet their fate by singing the jolly ditty "Always Look on the Bright Side of Life."

While critical appraisal was mostly positive, *Monty Python's Life of Brian* managed to generate negative comments by clergy members of different faiths. When it opened in New York, nuns picketed the theater and Rabbi Abraham Hecht, president of the Rabbinical Alliance of America, told *Variety*: "Never have we come across such a foul, disgusting, blasphemous film before." In the U.K., John Cleese and Michael Palin defended the film against charges of blasphemy on the BBC2 discussion program *Friday Night, Saturday Morning* featuring opposition from evangelical writer Malcolm Muggeridge and Mervyn Stockwood, the Bishop of Southwark.

Terry Gilliam reacted to the backlash with amusement. "I thought at least getting the Catholics, Protestants and Jews all protesting against our movie was fairly ecumenical on our part," he said. The governments of Ireland and Norway banned the film, but the latter provoked a snarky response from Sweden, where it was advertised as being "so funny it was banned in Norway."

But the controversy made no impact on the film's box office appeal. *Monty Python's Life of Brian* was the U.K.'s fourth highest grossing film in 1979, and it was the highest grossing British film in North American theatrical release for that year. In 2016, *Empire* magazine ranked it second on a list of the 100 best British films, with only David Lean's *Lawrence of Arabia* ranking higher.

And while the Pythons would always insist that *Monty Python's Life of Brian* was not a direct comic assault on Jesus, the success of the production would later embolden filmmakers who sought to approach the subject in a manner that veered closer to the profane than the sacred.

Pushing the Envelope with Jesus

Jesus would next appear on screen in a very brief sight-gag within Mel Brooks' splattery 1981 *History of the World, Part 1*, with John Hurt's Jesus posing for Art Metrano's Leonardo da Vinci painting the Last Supper – Brooks plays a rambunctious waiter at the meal and his intrusive presence behind Jesus is captured on canvas by the artist. In a film that was pockmarked with crass and tasteless humor, this sequence was the most sedate that Brooks conceived.

Jean-Luc Godard flirted with the subject in his 1985 *Hail Mary*, which transported the Nativity story into a modern setting. Godard's decision to have leading lady Myriem Roussel appear in full-frontal nudity raised ire in some quarters, most notably in a condemnation issued by Pope John Paul II, but the production was mostly acknowledged by critics as yet another entry in Godard's chronically iconoclastic canon while a spotty U.S. distribution via the art house circuit ensured that most Americans would not have access to its theatrical release. In 1986, the experimental *Jesus – Der Film* consisted of 35 short episodes made by a collective of 22 East and West German filmmakers working on Super 8 film. The film often had the off-kilter expressionistic style of the avant-garde experimental works from the 1920s and 1930s, but the work was barely seen.

The next Jesus-centric film that dared to offer a dramatic revision of the sacred story was Martin Scorsese's 1988 *The Last Temptation of Christ*. The director would state that he had been pursuing this project since actress Barbara Hershey gave him a copy of the Nikos Kazantzakis novel in 1972 during the production of his film *Boxcar Bertha*. Scorsese was not able to obtain the rights to the book until the late 1970s – Sidney Lumet tried but failed to adapt the work into a workable screenplay – but there was little interest from the major Hollywood studios until Paramount agreed to greenlight a film version in 1983 with a $14 million budget. But the project was cancelled when Scorsese's budget threatened to go further than its original parameters and fundamentalist Christian groups successfully lobbied the studio not to allow Kazantzakis' work to be filmed.

What was the problem with the source material? Kazantzakis, who published his book in 1951, set his story at the tail end of Jesus' pre-ministry days when He was still working in his family's carpentry business. His main clients are the Roman occupying force and he is paid to craft the massive wooden crosses used to fatally torture Jewish prisoners. This Jesus is despised by most of his community as a Roman collaborator, and even his old friend Judas Iscariot and the village prostitute Mary Magdalene have little use for him.

While this occurs, Jesus is haunted by dreams regarding God's plan for Him on Earth. With great reluctance and initial wobbliness in His public oratory, Jesus starts His Ministry. Of course, He is eventually convicted and sentenced to death by Pontius Pilate, but in this story a female angel enables the crucified Jesus to descend from the cross and live out the remainder of His life married to Mary Magdalene and, upon her death, in a polygamous union with the sisters Mary and Martha. As His life comes to a natural ending, Jesus realizes that the escape from cross was not God's will and the angel that liberated him from being crucified was actually Satan trying one last attempt at tempting Jesus away from the divine mission. Jesus manages to return to Golgotha and begs God to allow Him to complete the preordained mission – and Jesus finds himself back on the cross to die in order to save mankind.

Kazantzakis' book had the unique knack of uniting many of the faithful within the Catholic, Protestant and Eastern Orthodox religions into a common ground of denunciation. Despite the negative publicity surrounding Paramount's dumping of the project, Scorsese managed to convince Universal Pictures to accept the project. The studio agreed, but with the caveat that it be made on a $7 million budget, which was half the amount Paramount was willing to commit to. Scorsese was also limited to a two-month shooting schedule in Morocco.

Lacking the time and money to create a larger scale film, Scorsese eschewed the traditional grand spectacle of the Biblical epic to create a gritty drama that placed less emphasis on production design and more on character development and personality. This was hardly an original idea, as Pasolini already jettisoned the need for an epic production in his 1965 *The Gospel According to St. Matthew*. But whereas

Pasolini used the Gospel text for his screenplay, Scorsese worked from the Kazantzakis novel via a screenplay by Paul Schrader that was retooled by the director in collaboration with critic-turned-screenwriter Jay Cocks. And that's where things began to go awry.

The screenplay used for *The Last Temptation of Christ* carries a late-80s vibe that is too colloquial for its own good, with characters who behave like the thugs of Scorsese's crime dramas. This is particularly the case with Judas Iscariot, played by Harvey Keitel inexplicably wearing a red curly wig – where early in the film he violently smacks around Willem Dafoe's Jesus for not leading a rebellion against Rome. It is hard to decide whether to laugh, groan or walk away from the film. This is almost topped by Mary Magdalene as embodied by Barbara Hershey – her casting was obviously Scorsese's thanks for alerting him to the source material. She initially spits in Jesus' face for His work with Rome and later berates him when He visits her one-woman brothel but fails to make use of her services. At the other end of the spectrum, the traditionally bellicose John the Baptist is presented as a philosophical elder eager to discuss theology in an academic manner. As played by Andre Gregory, this is the mildest John the Baptist in movie history.

As for Willem Dafoe, the constant neurotic doubting that he channels into this Jesus was clearly intended to emphasis the human elements of His behavior. But the problem is that Dafoe under Scorsese's direction goes too far in jettisoning Jesus' divinity. This is a weak, often indecisive Jesus who acts like a constant victim of circumstance – it feels like every day in this Jesus' life is a Gethsemane-level anguish. At one point, Dafoe's Jesus remarks, "I'll just open my mouth, and God will do the talking," as if Jesus was little more than a dummy for a ventriloquist deity. This Jesus later complains, "God only talks to me a little at a time. He only tells me what I need to know" – this only makes Jesus seem like a clueless pawn in a grand chess game.

As the film plods along in its 163-minute running time, Dafoe's Jesus becomes less interesting and, quite frankly, more boring. As a result, the only entertainment one can plumb from the film are the occasional off-beat star cameos such as David Bowie as Pontius

Pilate and Harry Dean Stanton as the apostle Paul in the film's final dream sequence.

The controversy that the Monty Python funnymen generated for their film was mild compared to the reaction that Scorsese generated. The director received death threats and needed to hire private security when he was out in public. An extremist Catholic group set fire to a Paris theater that screened the film in October 1988, and boycott campaigns were organized in the U.S. Universal Pictures tried to calm the growing tide of anger against the production by arranging a private screening for fundamentalist leaders, but those who attended the screening were revolted by what was on the screen. A protest was held in front of the home of Lew Wasserman, then chairman of MCA, the parent company of Universal Pictures, and police intervention was required to quell the mob.

Universal Pictures inserted a card at the film's beginning reminding viewers that the film was based on a work of fiction, but that didn't appease anyone. Three different North American theater chains refused to exhibit the film and Blockbuster Video would not sell the home entertainment version when it was released in 1989. Several countries would not allow the film to be shown, including Mexico, Greece and Argentina. The Hollywood elite made a minimal attempt to rally behind this endeavor, granting Scorsese a nomination for the Academy Award as Best Director while Barbara Hershey and score composer Peter Gabriel snagged Golden Globe nominations. The film's low budget enabled it to record a small profit despite the problems related to its release.

Jesus in the Filipino and New York Jungles

A more intriguing attempt to retell the life of Jesus emerged in the Philippines in 1996 with *Kristo*, which greeted its audience by offering this remarkable prologue: "If the story of the New Testament replaced the setting from the Middle East to the Philippine Islands, what would the image and culture of the New Testament look like?"

The result, as depicted in *Kristo*, is a bizarre mix of ancient Judea and the Classical Filipino culture prior to the Spanish invasion and colonization in the 16th century. In this production, centurions in Roman uniforms and Sanhedrin chieftains in a vague approximation of Jewish prayer robes share the screen with people dressed in historic Filipino clothing. Sometimes, the Pacific Rim culture trumps the story's Middle Eastern roots, particularly in the sensual Filipino music and hip-swinging dances for the Wedding at Cana and Salome's wild dance for Herod Antipas.

Kristo has its roots in the traditional Filipino Passion Play that gets staged during Holy Week, and director Ben Yalung doesn't allow the material to fully make the transition from live theater to the big screen. This is obvious in a lot of the make-up, with patently phony beards and wigs that might be acceptable to audiences sitting hundreds of feet from a stage but which only inspire giggles when magnified one-hundred-fold on the screen. The film's low budget is also obvious in its few attempts at special effects, such as a badly animated dove descending from the sky during Jesus' baptism and the shoddy earthquake effect when Jesus expires on the cross.

But at the same time, Yalung is able to use the cinematic medium to achieve some startling emotional impacts. This is particularly evident when Jesus is tempted by Satan, who is initially depicted as a demure woman wearing a pink robe – a significant departure from the usual cinematic Satan that gives the temptation an added sexual vibe rather than a purely intellectual challenge, which could be considered alarming for some traditionalists, particularly when Satan acknowledges the futility of this action and is abruptly revealed to be an anything-but-demure male.

Equally impressive is the exorcism of Legion and the raising of Lazarus – in both scenes, those impacted by the miracle react with a gut-wrenching emotionalism that goes beyond mere acting. Aga Muhlach as the possessed man freed of his demons and Suzette Ranillo and Maureen Mauricio as Mary and Martha invest a heartbreaking depth into their relatively brief roles, crying out powerfully in tearful joy as their suffering is erased through unprecedented acts. Rez Cortez' Judas is equally jolting when expressing the remorse of his action, collapsing in near-hysteria when realizing what his betrayal has created. All of these actors achieve a state of anguish that is genuinely heartbreaking.

Yalung also presents a harsh Passion that goes beyond earlier Jesus-centric films, taking the torture of Jesus to a sadism that is eons removed from mere physical punishment – one has to wonder if Mel Gibson was aware of this film's level of brutality when preparing his blood-drenched *The Passion of the Christ*.

Mat Ranillo III plays Jesus in a forceful personality – he is a charismatic actor who generated authority with his presence. He is a no-nonsense Jesus, presenting the Sermon on the Mount in a straightforward manner and presenting miracles with a harsh seriousness. In the Passion, Ranillo essays Jesus' suffering with uncommon brilliance.

As with the majority of films made in the Philippines, *Kristo* is mostly unknown outside of its country. It does not appear that it was ever screened in the U.S., and the only way Americans can view it today is by a somewhat blurry and subtitle-free unauthorized posting on YouTube. While this is hardly the ideal way to appreciate *Kristo*, it represents an important link in how the cinema considered the Gospels, and its distinctive style makes it stand out from many less-than-stellar films made in the West.

At the tail end of the 20th century, independent filmmaker Hal Hartley tossed off an insouciant *The Book of Life* about Jesus (played by Martin Donovan) returning to Earth via New York City at the end of the millennium with his personal assistant Magdalena (P.J. Harvey) to determine whether the time is right to unleash the apocalypse on the world. The 1998 film only ran 63 minutes, which limited its exhibition to film festivals. Hartley packed the film with his trademark dry wit – Jesus contacts Satan via cell phone and announces Himself with a simple "It's me!" – but the film ultimately became more notable for being among the earliest productions by a major filmmaker to be shot on digital video rather than 35mm or 16mm film.

Willem Dafoe as Jesus in Martin Scorsese's 1989 The Last Temptation of Christ.

Chapter Six: 21st Century Jesus

"Jesus Christ is the same yesterday and today and forever."
— Hebrews 13:8

As cinema transitioned into the 21st century, filmmakers were challenged to find different ways to portray the often-told story of Jesus in a manner that did not replicate the style and substance of the previous century's films. The Hollywood studios recalled the controversy created with Martin Scorsese's *The Last Temptation of Christ* and were not eager to spark a new wave of ill will by deviating wildly from the sacred text. The growing wave of independent producers focused on evangelical Christian audiences lacked the financial power to coordinate old-school Biblical epics, focusing instead on contemporary features that advocated Christian principles.

The Miracle Maker spanned the 20th and 21st centuries, making its premiere in November 1999 as a Welsh-language direct-to-video release before appearing as an English-language version in British theaters in March 2000; the U.S. release in 2000 was as a television broadcast while Irish, French and Italian audiences first saw it in theaters.

An American-British-Russian co-production, *The Miracle Maker* had the unique distinction of being the first animated feature film on the life of Jesus, mixing stop-motion and hand-drawn animation. The English-language release has a stellar line-up of voice actors, with Ralph Fiennes as Jesus and an ensemble including Julie Christie, Miranda Richardson, William Hurt, Ian Holm, Alfred Molina and Daniel Massey. However, the 90-minute running time resulted in a significantly narrowed story and, to be cruel, the animation isn't particularly remarkable.

Jesus first turned up on 21st century U.S. movie screens via a film festival-distributed short called *Jesus and Hutch*, which reinvented the Man from Nazareth as a 1970s-style urban crime fighter. Eric Stoltz was the gun-toting, miscreant-chasing Jesus who inspires

Jim Caviezel as Jesus in Mel Gibson's The Passion of the Christ *(2004).*

the wicked to turn the other cheek with a left hook to the jaw. Even at four minutes, this 2000 film wore out its welcome before the closing credits. Two feature-length films also put Jesus in zany contemporary situations: the Canadian *Jesus Christ Vampire Hunter* (2001) conflated Jesus with the Van Helsing character from Bram Stoker's *Dracula* and the New York City-lensed *Ultrachrist!* (2001), which reinvented Jesus as a spandex-clad superhero.

A more mature and ambitious effort came in 2003 with *The Gospel of John*, a Canadian production that offered a verbatim adaptation of the American Bible Society's Good News Bible translation of the fourth Gospel. The film ran three hours and, excluding the silent presence of Mary Magdalene at the Last Supper, offered no additions from the other three gospels.

The problem with *The Gospel of John* is a wall-to-wall narration by Christopher Plummer. While this adheres to the format of a word-for-word filming of the text, it becomes burdensome and intrusive when describing actions that are evident to the viewer. As the Nazarene, Henry Ian Cusick is one of the happiest Jesuses in film history, going through much of His preaching with a can-do attitude and a comforting smile. It is a departure from the solemn and somber Jesuses of earlier historical dramas, and Cusick comes across like the rare Jesus who genuinely loves His work.

THINKFilm, the U.S. distributor for this work, appeared to have little faith in the production's commercial value and limited the release of *The Gospel of John* primarily to theaters in Bible Belt states. Its U.S. box office was a disappointing $4 million and it was barely acknowledged in the mainstream media. The film's subsequent release in home entertainment formats brought it before wider audiences, where viewer appreciation has been more substantial.

The Blood-Soaked Jesus

In 2004, the genre received a jolt from an unlikely source. Mel Gibson, who secured his international movie stardom in the *Mad Max* and *Lethal Weapon* franchises, had proven his worth as a filmmaker with the 1995 *Braveheart*, winning Academy Awards for

Best Picture and Best Director. Gibson was no stranger to Jesus-centric films – his Icon Productions was one of the companies that backed the aforementioned animated feature *The Miracle Maker* – and the financial success he secured from his movies enabled him to independently finance his own feature on Jesus. And working without studio interference, he intentionally went in creative directions that were never traveled by earlier filmmakers.

For starters, Gibson wanted to retell Jesus' experience in the languages of ancient Judea. After collaborating on a screenplay with Benedict Fitzgerald, he contracted William Fulco, a professor at Loyola Marymount University, to translate the work into Latin, Hebrew and a reconstructed version of the Aramaic that would have been spoken in Jesus' time.

Focusing on the last 12 hours of Jesus' life, Gibson culled the four Gospels but also added the Marian apparitions attributed to the nun Anne Catherine Emmerich (1774 – 1824), which were compiled into two books by the poet Clemens Brentano. These books sparked intense debate within the Roman Catholic Church, but Gibson followed an ultra-conservative branch of Catholicism that rejected the reforms of the Second Vatican Council, including the 1965 decree declaration "Nostra Aetate" that denounced anti-Semitism and formally rejected the accusation of deicide against the Jewish people for Jesus' death.

By concentrating on the circumstances that resulted in Jesus' death, Gibson opted to place a brutal realism to the physical torture that Jesus underwent. The result was a harsh and bloody consideration of how Jesus' body was torn apart during the scourging by Roman soldiers, tested further by carrying the cross through Jerusalem's streets and finally subjected to the intense agony of being nailed to the cross and crucified until dead. Prior to this film, there had not been a big screen Jesus who suffered so mightily and so painfully.

As a result of these creative decisions, Gibson's film *The Passion of the Christ* turned out to be among the most eccentric mainstream Jesus-centric films ever made. Part of the problem was Gibson's mania for artistic flourishes, ranging from a seemingly endless number of slow-motion shots to the unsubtle inclusion of an androgynous Satan

appearing throughout the film as a quiet manipulator of the tragedy that unfolds.

Gibson also took significant liberties with several of the characters in the story, starting almost immediately when the temple
guards who arrest Jesus at Gethsemane and throw him off a bridge.
Judas' motive for betrayal is never explained, but the remorse he
suffers for his action is compounded by having him tormented by
a group of violent children who chase him out of the Jerusalem.
Pilate's wife, called by her non-canonical name Claudia, is not only
an active advocate before her husband on behalf of Jesus, but goes
one step further by identifying Mary in the crowd after His scourging and giving her thick white towels to wipe the blood from the
ground left from the sadistic punishment. On the road to Calvary,
Jesus is joined by the two thieves who will be crucified alongside
him – both men carry their own crosses and bicker between each
other while insulting Jesus – and the non-canonical Veronica also
shows up to soak His image onto a cloth. But in this film, Simon
of Cyrene becomes so irritated by the crowd's abuse of Jesus that
he puts down the cross and berates all around him to knock it off
– the Roman soldiers are initially amused by this temper tantrum
but agree to restore order and let the procession continue without
the crowd's input.

Gibson shot his film in Italy, using a mix of European actors for
most of the roles – outside of Monica Bellucci as Mary Magdalene,
most of the cast were not familiar to U.S. audiences. Jim Caviezel,
a Hollywood actor who headlined a number of well-regarded dramas, was tapped to play Jesus. While Caviezel did an admirable
job emoting the physical suffering that Jesus underwent during the
Passion, Gibson's screenplay failed to offer evidence of how Jesus
could have made such an intellectual and emotional impact. One
flashback had a pre-ministry Jesus constructing an oversized table
at his family's carpentry shop, much to His mother's bafflement
– Gibson presented a playful Jesus who seemed like a completely
different person than the serious preacher. Flashbacks to the Sermon on the Mount and the Last Supper were crafted in such a flat
manner that Caviezel displays no charisma or authority in his role.
Indeed, by the time Pilate openly wondered why Jesus is creating

such a furor among the Sanhedrin chieftains, Cavaziel's Jesus was so close to being a blank slate that one could share the Roman governor's confusion.

But if Gibson's filmmaking could be debated, his promotional skills needed to be admired. Rarely was a film marketed with such aggressive gusto as *The Passion of the Christ*, with Gibson coordinating advance screenings for U.S. evangelical leaders, the heads of several mainstream Protestant faiths, and Pope John Paul II. The papal audience resulted in a controversy over whether the Pope approved of the film, with initial reports by *Wall Street Journal* columnist Peggy Noonan claiming John Paul II reacted to the film by saying "It is as it was" and other reporting calling that claim false.

But the accuracy of the papal quote paled to the charges of anti-Semitism within Gibson's work. The backlash to Gibson's perceived anti-Semitism actually began before the film released, when the Anti-Defamation League and several Jewish leaders called out Gibson and his work without having seen the finished film.

Compared to other films in this genre, *The Passion of the Christ* put a considerable emphasis on the role of Caiaphas and his fellow Sanhedrin leaders' role in Jesus' persecution, with Pilate demoted to a weakling easily bullied by the Jewish religious leaders. Caiaphas also showed up at Calvary to ensure Jesus has been crucified and will die: another artistic liberty. The original director's cut included Caiaphas bellowing the line from Matthew: "His blood be on us and on our children" – a quote that was justified for anti-Semitic persecution by Christians for centuries. Gibson initially promised to remove the line to appease objections raised by Jewish leaders, but reneged and kept it intact, only removing the English subtitle while the line was proclaimed in an Aramaic-language proclamation that contemporary audiences would not recognize.

The controversies surrounding the film dominated the news for weeks before the film opened and continued in the weeks after its premiere. Not surprisingly, this piqued the interest of movie audiences, and Gibson's efforts paid off handsomely – the $30 million *The Passion of the Christ* grossed $612 million, making it the most profitable film inspired by Jesus' life.

Mary Magdalene in the Spotlight

Into the 2000s, Mary Magdalene was given a chance to take center stage in a trio of films. This was not the first time the long-maligned Biblical figure was given her own film – the 1958 low-rent Italian production *La Spade e La Croce* (released stateside in 1960 as *Mary Magdalene*) created a delirious reimagining of Mary Magdalene's life that conflated her with the woman accused of adultery as well as being the sibling of Lazarus. Glamorous Hollywood star Yvonne De Carlo looked great in Mary Magdalene's form-fitting costumes, and that's about the only thing to recommend on that work.

As for the three modern Mary Magdalene films, none found a wide commercial audience despite their spirited efforts to reconsider the Biblical figure's role in Jesus's ministry.

Abel Ferrara, who made a reputation for helming gritty urban dramas including *Ms .45* (1981), *King of New York* (1990) and *Bad Lieutenant* (1992), seemed like an odd choice to direct a Biblical film. However, the iconoclastic filmmaker's eccentricities were on full display with *Mary*, which placed the Gospels within a troubled film production with Matthew Modine playing a writer/director who casts himself as Jesus. The eponymous character is Juliette Binoche as Mary Magdalene in the film-within-the-film and as a spiritually conflicted actress when out of her ancient Judean costume. Forest Whittaker, Heather Graham and Marion Cotillard gave the film extra star power.

In a rather salty interview with *Filmmaker* magazine, Ferrara admitted he came to *Mary* with minimal education on religious history.

"I knew very little," he said. "I mean, I'd read the Gnostic Gospels but that's the great thing about making films is that you get down to the subject. It's not a course in fuckin' required credit at university, you just get into it, it's your job to really understand it. *The Da Vinci Code* was the biggest selling book in the world, the Gibson movie was the biggest movie ever made and he had to make that with his own money. He distributed that with his own money.

Whatever you think of that movie, the motherfucker rocked the world. He rocked the fuckin' world."

Mary had an award-winning premiere at the 2005 Venice International Film Festival, but was not shown in a U.S. theatrical release until 2008 when Ferrara, unable to secure a distributor, arranged for a screening at New York's Anthology Film Archives. To date, the film has yet to be released on a U.S. DVD label and remains one of the colorful director's most obscure works.

In 2007 *Magdalena: Released from Shame* was released by the Jesus Film Project, the Campus Crusade for Christ subsidiary that created the 1979 *Jesus*. This film offered Mary Magdalene as both the narrator and the participant of her life's story. Footage of Brian Deacon as Jesus from the 1979 film was used for flashback sequences, with Rebecca Ritz in the title role.

As with *Jesus*, *Magdalena: Released from Shame* was barely acknowledged in the U.S. theatrical market, but its creators intended the work to be positioned for international nontheatrical distribution as a tool to spread the Christian message – particularly in countries where gender equality is mostly nonexistent.

"*Magdalena* has already been shown in other parts of the world where women encounter violence and humiliation simply because of their gender," said Jim Green, executive director of the Jesus Film Project, in an interview with the online news site *Christian Post*. "After test screenings in the United States we discovered that the *Magdalena* film can also be a very effective way to reach women here who may have never before considered the relevance of having Jesus in their lives."

The third film in this mini-genre was *Mary Magdalene* (2018) from Australian director Garth Davis, which offered a revisionist spin on the Biblical woman's life, presenting her as a forerunner of contemporary feminists who tried to achieve gender equality in an ancient male-dominated society. At one point, she attempts to break a taboo by praying alongside men in a synagogue; later, she flees from an arranged marriage and seeks an independent life in an environment where independent women were very few and far between. Mary becomes inspired by Joaquin Phoenix's Jesus and absorbs His teachings while later spreading His message after He has left the world.

Mary Magdalene was originally announced as a 2017 release from The Weinstein Company, but its premiere was delayed twice and eventually dropped by the distributor as company chieftain Harvey Weinstein found himself at the center of a massive sexual harassment controversy. IFC Films eventually picked up the film for a 2019 U.S. release – it had already played elsewhere in the world during 2018 – but mixed reviews and an indifferent promotional effort ensured a poor commercial return.

A fourth Mary Magdalene film was supposed to be made in Lebanon in 2009, marking the first time that the life of Jesus was the subject of a production from an Arab nation. Samir Habchi, director of the acclaimed 2008 work *Beirut Open City*, was announced as the creative force to helm *The Resurrected*, which was designed to tell Jesus' life in flashbacks through Mary Magdalene's perspective. Although news of the project was reported in international media outlets, the film was never made.

Bro Jesus

In some 21st century films, the resulting effort depicted Jesus as a "bro" – someone you could follow for gaining spiritual insight, but also someone who was the coolest dude in the room.

Spanish filmmakers Adrián Cardona and David Muñoz gave audiences a modern kick-ass Nazarene in the 2012 short *Fist of Jesus*, with the title character showing martial arts skills when the raising of Lazarus accidentally triggers a zombie apocalypse. Jesus and his sidekick Judas save the world from the undead. The short was originally planned as a teaser for a proposed feature, but attempts to crowdfund a budget for a longer production were unsuccessful.

Christopher Spencer's *Son of God* (2014) offered a pop star-worthy Jesus in the presence of Portuguese actor Diogo Morgado, who might have been the best-looking Jesus in film history – the actor inspired the social media tag #HotJesus. Morgado may not have been a great dramatic force – most of his performance alternates between cheery smiles and pensive frowns – but it becomes quickly obvious that his decorative presence outweighed his thespian limitations. *Toronto Sun* critic Jim Slotek noted the star's excessive good looks by quipping, "This really makes it unnecessary for Judas to kiss Jesus for identification purposes. Just arrest the handsomest guy you see."

Spencer's ancient Judea has a strangely contemporary feel to it: Mary Magdalene is front and center as a key member of the Apostles, children greet the Nazarene's arrival in their village by squealing "It's Jesus!" and a sour Pharisee trolls Jesus when He pauses to perform a miracle or offer a profound insight. The film does a casual rewrite of the Gospels by having Pilate as a hedonist who enjoys massages, lies around with his gorgeous wife while munching on grapes, and aggressively practices swordplay with muscular gladiators – the latter sequence, with its erotically charged energy, will certainly spark a few pings on viewers' gaydar that this Pilate happily swings both ways.

Son of God was carved out of a wider 10-hour History Channel miniseries called *The Bible*, with some material edited for the big screen presentation – most notably the removal of Jesus' temptation after some writers wondered if the film's Satan looked a little too much like then-President Barack Obama. Audiences did not mind paying to see a film that already received television airtime – an aggressive marketing campaign aimed at evangelical Christians made the film a vibrant box office hit.

Kevin Reynolds' *Risen* (2016) brought a more pronounced contemporary vibe to the Gospels. This film invented the Roman Tribune Clavius (played by Joseph Fiennes), who is tasked by Pilate to supervise the Crucifixion and to ensure Jesus is solidly sealed in the tomb. When the tomb is discovered to be empty and Jesus' body is gone, Clavius plays detective to locate Jesus' Disciples and, perhaps, recover the missing body.

Of course, the mystery of the disappeared body is solved in a manner that Clavius cannot fathom, with the resurrected Jesus (played by New Zealand Maori actor Cliff Curtis) gathered with his followers. But there is very little solemnity in the reunion of Jesus and the Apostles – everyone is laid back and laughing, having a grand old time. *Risen* is the rare film where Jesus and the Apostles behave like a group of buddies who enjoy each other's company – their gathering is not a movement in solemnity, but a guys' night out.

As with *Son of God*, movie audiences were willing to take a looser and lighter approach to the sacred texts and *Risen* was a commercial success during its theatrical release.

And then, there is *The Shack*, Stuart Hazeldine's 2017 adaptation of the best-selling novel by Canadian writer William Paul Young. *The Shack* is unique in presenting Jesus not as a single entity, but one of three entities personifying the Trinity. It also offers Jesus as a modern-age mindfulness coach, giving uplifting and insightful pep talks to help a troubled soul.

The central focus of *The Shack* is Mack (played by Sam Worthington), whose childhood was defined by a physically and emotionally abusive alcoholic father – Mack brought an end to this suffering when he was 13 years old by poisoning his father. Fast-forward to adulthood and Mack is a surprisingly well-adjusted adult with a loving wife and family, but tragedy strikes when one of his young daughters is kidnapped during a camping trip by a psychopath that the police identify as a long-elusive serial killer.

The disappearance of his daughter causes Mack to lose his religious faith, but a mysterious unsigned note that appears in his mailbox encourages him to come to a vacant cabin in the woods where his daughter's bloodstained dress was found. Mack goes to the cabin and finds it vacant. Distraught, he takes the gun he is carrying and readies it for a suicidal shot when three strangers – a Black woman, a Middle Eastern man and an Asian woman – appear and invite him to their adjacent home, which is based in an impossibly lush forest.

In the strangers' home, Mack is dumbfounded to discover the identity of his hosts. The Black woman, who is the most forceful personality of the trio (Octavia Spencer), is revealed to be God, while the Middle Eastern man (Aviv Alush) is Jesus and an Asian woman identified as Sarayu (Japanese model/actress Sumire Matsubara).

For the remainder of the film, this trio works carefully – sometimes in unison, sometimes separately – to help Mack regain his faith and to tend to the emotional scars that burden him through a series of quasi-mystical conversations that are closer in spirit to psychoanalysis than Scriptures. Mack's solo sessions with Jesus (who favors a plaid shirt and jeans) take place along a pristine lake in a buddy-bonding exercise – Mack is initially rowing a boat when the water becomes tumultuous. And, of course, who should come walking out on the water but Jesus? To his amazement, Mack is escorted by Jesus to walk on the water back to the shore.

Mack has problems with the concept of Jesus as a friendly contemporary dude and remarks, "You don't really fit all of the religious stuff I was taught." Jesus laughs and responds, "Religion? Religion is way too much work. I don't want slaves. I want friends – family to share your life with."

Jesus – whose wrists show the faint scars created in the Crucifixion – then adds, "Think about it, Mack. I'm not exactly what you would call Christian." Later, the two engage in a friendly foot race across the lake's surface.

The film complicates things further when God is somehow transitioned into a Native American male (Graham Greene) who helps Mack track down his daughter's dead body. Jesus employs His pre-ministry carpentry skills to build a handsome coffin that enables Mack to bury his child with dignity. The spirit of Mack's dead father shows up to provide belated forgiveness for his son's poisoning and for the actions that drove the young Mack to patricide. In the end, Mack's odyssey turns out to be – what else? – a dream.

Aviv Alush plays Jesus as a wise best friend to Sam Worthington's Mack, but the latter spends so much of the film looking about confused at what is occurring that their relationship often becomes unintentionally funny. The main thrust of Mack's healing regimen involves Octavia Spencer's God, which leaves Alush's Jesus as a supporting member of this multicultural Trinity who competes with Sumire Matsubara's Holy Spirit for screen time.

When *The Shack* began to gain attention as a best-selling novel in 2017, it generated an intellectual controversy among theologians and commentators in religious media on its highly unorthodox interpretation of the Trinity. By the time *The Shack* was theatrically released 10 years after the book's publication, audiences were not offended by a production that took excessive liberties with the sacred material. Quite the opposite, actually – the movie turned out to be among the most commercially popular films of that year, while its soundtrack album topped the Christian music charts thanks to songs from major country music stars including Faith Hill and Tim McGraw (who had a small role in the film), Lady Antebellum and Dierks Bentley.

The Multicultural Jesus

By the end of the 20thcentury, the cinematic depiction was almost entirely in keeping with the appearance of the white men featured as Jesus in medieval and Renaissance European artwork – often with flowing blonde hair and blue eyes that were not particularly ubiquitous among the ancient Judean population. Even in films made in Asia and Mexico, the on-screen Jesus was inevitably cast by the lightest-skinned actors. (Despite its title, the 1968 Italian film *Black Jesus* starring the great character actor Woody Strode was a modern drama inspired by the murder of Congolese Prime Minister Patrice Lumumba and had nothing to do with the New Testament.)

Into the 21st century, filmmakers from around the world have sought to shift away from the Eurocentric concept of Jesus by attempting radical riff on the very familiar story.

Iranian director Nader Talebzadeh's 2007 *Mesih* (also known as *Jesus, the Spirit of God*) gained media attention for being the first from an Islamic country about Jesus and for dramatically reconfiguring the story by basing Jesus' ministry on the noncanonical Gospel of Barnabas. This source material adheres to a Quranic notion of Jesus by denying His divinity and foretelling the coming of Muhammad. Oddly, Talelzadeh adhered to the Renaissance artists' physical depiction of Jesus and had leading man Ahmad Soleimani Nia wear long blonde hair and an extravagant blonde beard.

The director was quoted in the press as saying he hoped *Mesih* would be able "to make a bridge between Christianity and Islam, to open the door for dialogue." However, the film was barely seen in the U.S. outside of a few very minor festivals, so any exchange of opinions, either meaningful or rancorous, never occurred.

A few Jesus-focused films from the Arab world have appeared in recent years: *The Savior*, a 2014 Palestinian-Jordanian-Bulgarian co-production shot in the Arabic language with Israeli actor Shredi Jabarin as Jesus; *Men Ajlikom* (*For You*), a 2015 Lebanese short film directed by the Carmelite Father Charles Sawaya and starring Chadi Haddad as Jesus Christ; and *Histoire de Judas* (2016), in which Algerian director Rabah Ameur-Zaïmeche reimagines Judas' relation with Jesus, who is played by Nabil Djedouani. However, these films never played in U.S. theaters

The clash between Islamic and Christian theologies was at the heart of Jim Carroll's 2020 release *Assassin 33 A.D.*, a science-fiction tale of American scientists chasing after Muslim extremists who use a time machine to go back to ancient Judea to assassinate Jesus before the Crucifixion, thus ensuring the course of history would be irrevocably changed. The few critics who saw the film denounced its racist content and incompetent production values, and audiences were mostly oblivious to its existence.

The Brazilian comedy group Porta dos Fundos sought to gain attention by creating two films that poked flippant fun at the Gospels. The first film, the 2018 *Especial de Natal Porta dos Fundos* (*The Last Hangover*), followed the Disciples who awaken with hangovers after the Last Supper to wonder what became of Jesus – this did not generate much anger among Brazilian viewers. But the follow-up, the 2019 *A Primeira Tentação de Cristo* (*The First Temptation of Christ*), which implied Jesus was a closeted homosexual while Mary was a marijuana addict, created controversy in Brazil when it was streamed on Netflix, resulting in attempts to have the nation's courts ban the film, and Porta dos Fundos' office in Rio de Janeiro was bombed with two Molotov cocktails. However, the films didn't raise a blip of controversy in the U.S., except for a few breathless news stories reporting on the Brazilian outrage.

In 2019, Indian director Aneek Chaudhuri screened *Cactus* at the Cannes Film Festival, starring Aparajita Dey as cinema's first adult female Jesus. (As cited earlier in this book, the infant Martha Friedrich was recruited as baby Jesus for the 1941 short *The Child of Bethlehem*.) Chaudhuri told the Indian newspaper *The Citizen* that he "cannot think of any male as the epitome of Christ, as depicted in Bible. The sensitivity, or the endurance, I strongly feel only a woman has such characteristics." Unfortunately for Chaudhuri, the film made little impact at Cannes and quickly fell off the radar.

One trend that seemed to gain more traction was having Jesus portrayed as a Black man. In 2006, two films were released that offered the first Black Jesuses in cinema history. First was the South African production *Son of Man*, which updated the Gospels into a contemporary sub-Saharan Africa setting. This modern Black Jesus (Andile Kosi) echoes the teachings of His ancient Judean counterparts, along with new complaints aimed at the avarice of profit-driven drug companies.

"Unrest is due to poverty, overcrowding, and lack of education," Jesus proclaims. "We must prove we're committed to nonviolent change; then negotiations can begin."

Later in the film, Jesus goes into a long rant that has nothing to do with the Gospels and everything to do with developing world politics.

"I'm not here to destroy beliefs and traditions but to create them anew," the film's Jesus states to His followers. "We must forgive those who offend us and those who trample on our comrades, otherwise our hatred will destroy our future. When those with imperial histories pretend to forget them, and blame Africa's problems on tribalism and corruption, while building themselves new economic empires, I say we have been lied to – evil did not fall. When I hear someone was beaten and tortured in the Middle East, I say we have been lied to – evil did not fall. When I hear that in Asia child labor has been legislated, I say we have been lied to – evil did not fall. When politicians in Europe and the USA defend trade subsidies and help restrict the use of medicine through commercial patents, I say we have been lied to – evil did not fall. When you are told, and you will be, that people just 'disappear,' you must say we have been lied to. And evil will fall."

Director Mark Donford-May worked in collaboration with the theater group Dimpho Di Kopane on this project. Some of the artistic choices are inspired, especially the use of South African music to frame the emotions of the scenes. Some choices are a bit fey: the film depicts angels as young boys with a few feathers glued to them, Satan is a sketchy character in a red t-shirt and a trench coat, and Judas' betrayal does not occur with a kiss, but with evidence recorded on a camcorder and presented to His persecutors.

Son of Man jettisoned the Sanhedrin and the distinctive challenge Jesus posed to the Jewish religious leadership, focusing instead on an African military government that views Jesus as a political threat. And Jesus' death occurs in a fatal beating at the hands of the military, with His body later placed by Mary on the cross after He has passed away.

Kosi, who goes through most of the film in jeans and a checkered shirt, is a handsome and charismatic Jesus, playing the role as more of a political organizer than a spiritual savior. Donford-May admitted his concept of Jesus was inspired in large part by Stephen Biko, the anti-apartheid activist who was beaten to death by security forces in 1977.

Son of Man was a popular title on the film festival circuit, earning a nomination for the Grand Jury Prize at the 2006 Sundance Film Festival, but commercial theatrical release was minimal and the film would only find a wider audience through DVD sales.

Jean Claude LaMarre, a Brooklyn-born actor/writer/director of Haitian heritage, cast himself as Jesus in his 2006 film *The Color of the Cross*. Set during the final 48 hours of Jesus' life, LaMarre added a radically different element to the story by placing the persecution of Jesus on both his race and his threat to the Sanhedrin power structure.

Throughout the film, Jesus' actions are defined by his race. Mary (played by Debbi Morgan) views the growing opposition by the powerful elite against her son and asks, "Do you think they are doing this because He is Black?" while the sympathetic religious elder Nicodemus ponders if "this dark-skinned Nazarene" could be the long-awaited Messiah. Even LaMarre's Jesus acknowledges his minority status by stating, "In my father's eyes, we are all different, yet we are all the same."

While LaMarre's message is sincere, it is also anachronistic to the point that it becomes unintentionally funny. This is especially evident when Peter attempts to save Jesus from arrest by claiming to be Him; a Roman centurion rejects the subterfuge by growling,

"You're not Black enough, Jew!" – nothing like stirring up racism and throwing in an anti-Semitic chaser. It also doesn't help that LaMarre's Jesus is mostly passive – almost somnambulistic – through most of the film, abruptly displaying a volcano of emotions in the Gethsemane scene.

LaMarre made his film on a $2.5 million budget that did not allow him the grandeur one associates with a Biblical production. As a result, much of the film is shot in close-ups and the cramped setting of the Last Supper occupies much of the running time. But with only 81 minutes in running time, *The Color of the Cross* is unable to expand on Jesus' experience – and in a very curious decision, LaMarre cuts abruptly from the arrest at Gethsemane (with Judas also played by a Black actor, Johann John Jean) to the Crucifixion. As a result, this gives the unfortunate expectation that the arresting party served double duty as executioners, with nary a mention of a trial before Pontius Pilate.

LaMarre generated a great deal of media attention with this production and 20th Century-Fox picked up the theatrical rights to *Color of the Cross*, perhaps in hope of lightning striking twice – the studio passed on the theatrical rights to Mel Gibson's *The Passion of the Christ* two years earlier, although it snagged the lucrative home entertainment release rights. But when early critical feedback was negative, the studio had a severe change of heart and *Color of the Cross* only played in 29 theaters across the U.S. during the peak of its brief and poorly promoted theatrical release. LaMarre managed to create a sequel, the 2008 *Color of the Cross 2: The Resurrection*, but no theatrical distributor was interested and it was released as a direct-to-DVD title.

Following the release of *Son of Man* and *Color of the Cross*, the notion of a Black Jesus was absent from the big screen for several years, but it started to appear more frequently on the small screen. A trash-talking Black Jesus was used for comic effect in a 2009 episode of the irreverent animated television series *Family Guy* while the 2014 Adult Swim series *Black Jesus* had the title character (played by comic and rapper Gerald "Slink" Johnson) living in modern-day Compton, California; the show ran for three seasons to good reviews and strong ratings, arousing no controversy.

The 2018 made-for-television production of *Jesus Christ Superstar Live in Concert* had Black singer/actor John Legend as Jesus – and with this production, no critic bothered to fixate over having a non-white performer cast as Jesus.

Also, in 2018, Grammy-nominated and GMA Dove Award-winning singer Mali Music took on the role of Jesus in *Revival!*, a wildly inventive production that brought a mostly original gospel and R&B music score and creative reinterpretations to the story. Directed by Danny Green and co-written by Harry Lennix and Holly Carter, *Revival!* injected a massive surge of energy into the genre, taking artistic risks and often succeeding in its audacity.

The film opens in a live theater setting with Lennix as the master of ceremony. The viewer is informed, "You are about to witness a timeless story, but perhaps not the way you expected to witness it." A montage of performers and orchestra members readying for a show is followed by Music coming into his dressing room, where he witnesses a ghostly image in the mirror. The actor and the vision in the mirror merge and take the story into ancient Judea, where the Disciples learn that Jesus' tomb has opened and His body is nowhere to be found. Mary Magdalene (played by former Destiny's Child member Michelle Williams) is the first to witness the resurrected Jesus and breaks into happy song.

The film then finds Jesus revealing Himself to the Disciples, and this is followed by having Jesus join a man and woman who are traveling to share His story. They don't recognize Him and He listens as they recount the ministry from its beginning at Cana. The rest of the film is told in flashback, with occasional cutaways to Jesus and the travelers.

Revival! offers a multiracial cast with modern language and a mix of ancient and contemporary settings to recall Jesus' ministry – the film switches between cinematic and theatrical effects, often in split-second transitions. Much of the film has a playfully flippant attitude – at Cana, for example, Jesus is expected by Mary to bring the wine to the ceremony.

The temptation by Satan is presented in a startling manner, with Satan divided into an unholy trinity. With the attempt to lure the hungry Jesus into food, Satan is shown as a wealthy gourmand at an overflowing table with champagne and chocolates. With the attempt to coerce Jesus to throw Himself from a great height, Satan is a boy sitting with Jesus atop one of the letters on Los Angeles' celebrated Hollywood sign. And with the attempt to bribe Jesus with worldly treasures, Satan is a sexy burlesque performer (brilliantly interpreted by Victoria Gabrielle Platt) who bumps and grinds and vamps her way around Jesus while a chorus gyrates around her efforts. "This is my house you're playing in!" she declares to Jesus. "And nobody beats the house!"

Purists might quibble with some liberties that the film takes in rearranging the chronology of the story – for example, the expulsion of the moneychangers from the temple comes early in the story – and the religious aspects of the story are somewhat confused with Jesus wearing a Star of David on his chest while an imperious female chieftain is presented as the driving force of Sanhedrin persecutors; the latter also makes the non-canonical suggestion that the Sanhedrin had Lazarus assassinated after he was brought back to life. And the role of Herodias is considerably expanded to enable a guest star turn by R&B legend Chaka Khan, who performs a sultry siren song to convince her royal spouse that John the Baptist needs to be taken out.

Not every effect in *Revival!* works – most notably an odd time-travel gimmick where Pilate is seen moving from a contemporary boardroom through various epochs until he reaches old Jerusalem. But more often than not, the effects are striking, particularly the theatrical setting where Jesus' walking on water is illustrated with billowing fabrics and inventive lighting, while the centurions' torture of Jesus is laced with lightning bolts that appear with each strike of the whip.

If there is one weakness in *Revival!* it would be in Music's performance as Jesus. Although he is a gifted singer and an invaluable aspect of the film's vibrant soundtrack, Music's dramatic presence is often flat and in too many scenes he comes across as a stiff observer to a jubilant ensemble. In what should have been his dramatic big scene in Gethsemane, his emoting never truly plumbs the anguish of Jesus' emotional torture. It is also a bit strange to have supporting actor Sebastian C. Besquet as Andrew made up to resemble the

Renaissance art interpretation of Jesus – while this could be seen as a challenge to common perception of what Jesus and the Disciples looked like, it becomes a strange distraction.

Revival! opened theatrically in the U.S. in December 2018 in only 10 theaters and was heavily marketed to an African-American audience, to the point where many white moviegoers were unaware of its presence. The film had a sparse theatrical run into 2019 and found wider audiences via streaming services and DVD sales.

In 2020, two more Black Jesus films emerged. Swiss filmmaker Milo Rau's Italian-lensed *The New Gospel* mixed the staging of a Passion Play against a modern story on the squalor and despair facing African migrants in Europe. Rau cast Yvan Sagnet, a Cameroonian activist and author with no previous acting experience, in the role of Jesus.

The New Gospel had its premiere at the 2020 Venice International Film Festival, which was a mostly virtual event due to the coronavirus pandemic. The European media was full of invigorating reports on how this film reanimated the religious film genre while offering a harshly honest consideration of migrant life in Europe. As of the writing of this book, the film has not received a U.S. theatrical premiere, although an English-subtitled trailer can be found on YouTube.

In the same year, Nigerian filmmaker Tchidi Chikere brought forth *Our Jesus Story*, with Frederick Leonard as Jesus. *Our Jesus Story*'s premiere in Nigeria, scheduled for March 27, 2020, was postponed due to the COVID-19 pandemic until December 12, 2020. As with Rau's film, Chikere's production did not cross the Atlantic for theatrical release when this book was completed, but an English-subtitled trailer on YouTube offers an intriguing mix on the ancient Judean story – with a level of Passion violence to rival Mel Gibson's work – and a contemporary morality tale set within modern Nigeria.

Clearly, the story of Jesus continues to inspire diverse and remarkable sources of creativity. To borrow a phrase from Isaiah, it is truly a world without end.

Yvan Sagnet as Jesus in Milo Rau's 2020 production The New Gospel.

Author's Acknowledgments

"May the Lord reward you for your kindness."
– Ruth 1:8

This book exists solely through the good graces and patient support of Ben Ohmart, publisher of Bear Manor Media. I am grateful to be among the writers whose work is published by Ben and his wonderful company.

Don Hogan and Stone Wallace deserve a shout out for copy editing my text. Some of the essays in this book appeared in an earlier version on the Cinema Crazed website, and I am thankful for my editor and publisher and dear friend Felix Vasquez Jr. for allowing me to use the website to preview and test my material.

Rev. Caleb Scott Evans contributed a brilliant foreword to this book, and I am grateful to have him as a collaborator on this project and as the pastoral leader of my faith family.

Inspiration, input and invigoration can be credited to these wonderful people, presented in alphabetical order: Robbie Adkins, Mark Arnold at *Fun Ideas Podcast*, Jeffrey Cintolo, Rich Cyr, Jack Holman, Sophia Lorent at the George Eastman Museum, Lisa Lyon at *Coast to Coast AM*, Doreen Madden, Joe Mannetti, Wakefield Poole, Zoran Sinobad of the Library of Congress, Clint Weiler and Martin Yates.

I need to cite three people who were in the right place at the right time during the course of my spiritual life. I can give special thanks to Prof. Lawrence Hundersmarck, my religious studies teacher at Pace University; Rev. William Davidson, the now-retired rector of Christ Church Riverdale in the Bronx, New York, my longtime religious home; and Rev. James Debner, former pastor at Zion Lutheran Church in Southington, Connecticut, who welcomed me into his faith community during a difficult time of my life.

I wish that my beloved grandmother, Beatrice Pam, and my friends Robin Lim, Joe Kane and Carmine Capobianco were here to share in this book's release, but they have gone on to a better world. While I enjoy my time on Earth today, I look forward to reuniting with them for eternity.

My extraordinarily patient mother Ruth Hall and my wonderfully rambunctious Bichon Frise brother Joshua Clancy Hall get an extra special shout out for putting up with me during the creation of this work – as well as dealing with me on a daily basis, which requires Job-worthy patience.

This book is a culmination of two very different passions in my life: the celebration of all things cinematic and my Christian faith. I hope that my attempt to unite these pursuits into a single work will please those who pick up this book.

About the Author

Phil Hall's three-decades-plus cinema/media career covers achievements as a film journalist, critic, publicist, distributor, festival programmer and actor. His books include *The History of Independent Cinema*, *The Greatest Bad Movies of All Time*, *In Search of Lost Films* and *The Weirdest Movie Ever Made: The Patterson-Gimlin Bigfoot Film* (all published by BearManor Media).

Hall's film-related writing has appeared in *The New York Times*, *New York Daily News*, *Hartford Courant*, *Wired*, *Film Threat* and the *Library of Congress'* website. He is also the host of the award-winning SoundCloud podcast *The Online Movie Show with Phil Hall*, the co-host of the award-winning radio show *Nutmeg Chatter*, an editor and columnist at the *Cinema Crazed* website, and a former member of the Online Film Critics Society's Governing Committee.

Hall graduated from Pace University with a major in journalism and a minor in religious studies. In the course of his career, he has also been a United Nations journalist for *Fairchild Broadcast News*, a financial journalist and editor, the co-host and producer of the long-running Internet radio show *PPRN Radio*, and an actor and playwright.

Index